The Hire Effect™

The Hire Effect™

Hiring for Culture and Skill

by

M. Miche Rayment

The Hire Effect™

Copyright © 2016 by M. Miche Rayment. All rights reserved. Printed in the United States of America. Except as permitted under the Copyright Act of 1976, no part of this publication may be reproduced or distributed in any form or by any means, or stored in a data base or retrieval system, without the prior written permission of the author.

For Spsisa

Contents

Oh the Pain of it All xi
Preface xiii
   THE Genesis xiii
   Much Gratefulness xv
Introduction 1
   What is The Hire Effect™? 1
      THE in Short 3
      Client Experience Asides 5
      Enlightened Leaders 7
THE Unconventional Hiring Team 9
   Roles on Your Hiring Team 11
      The Unconventional Hiring Team as a Whole 12
      The Decider 12
      The Team Member That Embodies the Culture 13
      Project Manager 14
      The New Employee's Manager 14
      A Peer of the New Employee 15
      An Intuitive Person 15
      An Individual with Vested Interest 16
   Conclusion 18
      Initial Actions 18
THE Right Fit™ 19
   Your Company Culture 21
      Core Values 23
      Manner 25
   Candidate Skills and Traits 28
      Skills 29
      Traits 31

Conclusion 32
Initial Actions 33
THE Obstacle Course 34
  Low Touch and High Touch 36
  Assignments 38
  Other Considerations and Supporting Documents of THE Obstacle Course 41
    Supporting Document | THE Obstacle Course Graphic .. 41
    Consideration | Assignments on Site and Necessity 42
    Supporting Document | Candidate Pool Tracking 42
    Consideration | How many steps to use 46
    Consideration | Strategies and Tactics for Interviewing .. 47
    Supporting Document | Assignments and Script Documents 50
    Consideration | Interview Script Design 52
    Consideration | Campaign Timeline 53
    Consideration | An Observation in Listening 53
    Consideration | Building a Good Candidate Pool 54
    Consideration | Constructing a Good Job Posting 56
  Conclusion 58
  Initial Actions 59
THE Proof 61
  Assertions and Assessments 63
    Assessments | Plus, Zero, Minus 64
    Making Core Values Assessments 68
    Making Manner Assessments 68
    Making Skill Assessments 70
    Making Trait Assessments 72

Considerations 75
   Consideration | What to Do About A Zero 75
   Consideration | Building an Onboarding Plan 76
  Conclusion 78
   Initial Actions 78
THE Higher Effect 79
   Consideration | A Compatible Leadership System 80
   Consideration | THE Team Assessment 84
   Consideration | Organizational Change 90
   Consideration | Seating Your Culture 92
  Conclusion 93
   Initial Actions 93
Wrap Up and Concluding Thoughts 95
Appendix A 98
Appendix B 99
Appendix C 100
Appendix D 101
Distinctions 103
Bibliography 107

Oh the Pain of it All

"Honestly I felt like throwing up. I'd just invested over $100K in hiring, training and getting him up to speed and one day three weeks in, he just quit."

"Every time I hire someone new I have this pit in my stomach. I'm waiting to find out if it actually pans out. Did I make another mistake?"

"She was great for about a week and then little things kept popping up that just didn't feel right. I ignored it because I desperately needed her to work out. Now I don't know what to do."

"The worst thing about it? He dragged down two of my best employees for a few months before I accepted the loss. What a mess that was."

"Whenever I have to stop what I'm doing and hire another person, I feel like I'm playing a high-stakes game of craps. Finding the right people just isn't my strong suit."

"The very first thing I do when I know I have to hire someone new is set up a regular prayer to begin each day. Although my faith is strong, I wish that wasn't the only thing I relied upon when a new person needs to join the team. I just don't want to make a mistake for everyone else's sake!"

"I feel like forming a huddle with the team and chanting … "We can do this! We can do this!" Unfortunately, positive thinking doesn't get us all the way, just part of the way."

"I kept hiring to fill a void, but I had no idea what that void actually was. We just keep doing more stuff so I hired people to do it. I've never had a real idea of what the gap on the team is."

"My employee turnover rate is nearly twice the industry standard. What the hell?! Someone please help me."

"They say to hire slow and fire fast. That's so much easier said than done especially when you need someone yesterday."

"I can see immediately what my customers need for the best event of their company's existence. The lighting, the staging, the sound—all amazing! Why can't I hire dependable people? It's so hit or miss."

Take a deep breath. There is a way for you to get better at hiring.

Preface

THE Genesis

Over half my life ago, while taking phone calls from irate Chevy owners, I started to see the true power of choosing who was on my team. I didn't know it then, but The Hire Effect™ (THE) was born in those grueling few years as a youngster. Who would I have on my team if I could choose from the other 250 people doing this sometimes-thankless job? It was pretty clear to me I wanted those that shared my core values and worked the way I worked. It was my own business culture I wanted them to fit.

As life progressed and we founded our consulting business, DCCI, in the early '90s, the culture was formed from those same values and manner of work—Integrity, Openness, and Forthrightness were our core values while Complete, Optimistic, Flexible, and Focused were the manners constructing the mood of the work at DCCI.

It was in the late '90s and early 2000s, knowing clearly what our culture was, that we hired using the principles put forth in this book. We didn't call it The Hire Effect and we didn't have the tools as they are now. We did, however, hire knowing what a cultural match looked like, put candidates through unusual paces to see how they would perform in that culture, and discussed at length what we saw, examining thoroughly how their performance fit what we needed and who we were.

THE came fully to life after I worked with many hundreds of startups and growth stage businesses through years of economic development consulting. One thing is for sure: at DCCI we had uncommonly loyal employees and an uncommonly good time working together. This is what I hope for everyone who implements THE in their own business—a loyal team and joy working together.

Much Gratefulness

There are many people to be grateful for in THE work. I am grateful for those incredibly supportive people in my life who were always willing to listen to a new part of THE, telling me to move on when my ideas had no merit and encouraging me when it had promise—Rosemary Bayer, Linda Teaman, Jeff Eusebio, Maria Kokas, Nicole Mangis, Rachele Downs, Diane Durance, Kevin Suboski, Angela Barbash, Mary Nickson, and Joe Sadler. I am equally grateful for those that helped me with the mechanics and puzzle piecing—William J. Rayment (who could be the only one to appreciate the title of the last section), Bonnie Dawdy, Ted Hutchins (Ladybird-Digital), Kristin Dawdy (Dawdy Imagery), Paige Wantuck, Hana Wantuck, Chaeli Wantuck, Tom Voiles, and Katrina Rayment.

I am grateful for those that are a part of me and reflect nearly daily on THE—Linda Teaman and Mo Horner. I would be remiss if I didn't thank those who are my mood buddies, reminding me of the delightful future ahead when I was down or verbally knocking some sense into me when I needed a pep talk— Christine Cross, Rosemary Bayer, Vicki Reid Smith, Casey Smith, Lenny Rayment, Tom Root, Julie and Mike Bellaw, Andrea and Matt Dahline, Angela Peat, and Terry Terry.

For infinite growth as a human I will always be grateful for my children Spencer, Simon, and Sarah Suboski, in addition to my parents Larry and Shirley Rayment—you all push me in ways you will never fully realize.

Introduction

What is The Hire Effect™?

As a small business owner, you are probably very good at producing your product or service. After all, it's your core competency. If you want to stay around or grow, though, you have to get equally good at hiring for yourself too. The Hire Effect™ (THE) will reduce your pain, anxiety and confusion over hiring and, if implemented properly, can get your turnover rate to become lower than you would imagine, build a great tight-knit team and give you more time to do the things at which you are brilliant.

The Hire Effect (THE) encompasses a coordinated dance of language, human systems and tools that ultimately results in constantly building a team to take your company into its future smoothly—this year, next year and many years from now.

Implementing and working with ***THE System***, the core of THE, ensures a coherent story that everyone on your team shares, right from the beginning, about what the team members need and how they'll spot the best candidate (and the ones who would be poison too). Although you will read more about this later, there is nothing more effective for your company than getting everyone using the same terminology *with the same meaning*. Business thrives in a shared language; you'll get what I mean soon.

Whenever you make choices (business or not), you need to do three things in order to choose well: know what you want, get good data, and get solid proof on your decision, rather than just relying on your intuition.

THE System includes a process for each of those things:

- Know what you want: ***THE Right Fit*** is a framework for outlining exactly what you want in the next employee filling a *role* in your company. Does the candidate fit your *culture*? Do they have the skills and personality to succeed in your company?

- Get tons of good data: **THE Obstacle Course** is a series of steps that candidates go through while your hiring team observes, getting data aplenty from candidates performing for you (good and bad). Are you *watching* the *doing* and *listening* to the *saying*, then comparing those results to THE Right Fit?

- Draw from solid proof: **THE Proof** is a set of tracking tools to support assessments you make during the interviewing process. Do you have a good way to check your gut? Are you and your team Blessing and Releasing? *More on that later.* Do you know what onboarding looks like for your best candidates before you offer them a job?

The three components listed above correspond with the major problems most business owners face when hiring: they can't clearly identify what an ideal candidate looks like for them from the standpoints of both skill and culture, they don't know how to get candidates to act or behave the way they would normally (rather than how they act in an interview process), and they don't know how to find real proof that the candidate fits what they truly want.

Tailoring THE System and implementing it well will also net you some other, unexpected benefits in the long run:

- Discover **THE Unconventional Hiring Team**: By delegating to and developing your current team to be responsible for hiring, then holding them accountable, you will introduce a shared-responsibility approach to your business that significantly increases successfully attracting, hiring, and retaining great talent.

- Clearly describe and apply **Your Business Culture** – You'll articulate your business culture and realize how you can leverage it to be more authentic, consistent and powerful, in the hiring process and other core business processes.

- Find another way of **Engaging and Developing Your Current Team**: THE principles set out in the following pages will provide a structure to discover what others in your company want and need in order to do a great job. Once you've engaged with your core team, you'll see how the rest of your employees, vendors and consultants can be engaged to produce even better results for everyone.

- Learn new tools to **Encourage Meaningful and Productive Conversations**: Presented herein are samples of tools THE clients use to coordinate their high performing teams. You'll discover how you could use them too.

- Be exposed to **Scripts** for your hiring process, both interview and communication scripts: Your team can construct interview and response scripts (there are examples a bit later) in the planning processes of your hiring campaign. Doing so will ensure that you treat candidates respectfully and consistently to get accurate data.

- Build a **Library of Assignments**: You will learn how to design and implement *assignments* then you'll create a databank of assignments as you move on to other hiring campaigns.

THE in Short

The Hire Effect offers a way for you and your team to gain the core competencies you need to hire for yourself. THE helps you get clear on who you are and what you need in a candidate, stick to process as you compare candidates, and work together to make a proven choice. And . . . you can do it without feeling like you are going to throw up, have to gather the team yet again for a cheerleading session, or rely on your faith to get you your next employee.

Client Experience Asides

Throughout this book you'll encounter *Client Experience* sections. These experiences will hopefully make it fun by shining a light on how people encounter the ideas and processes in this book.

Each one of the experiences has happened, sometimes multiple times with only slight variation. None of these experiences is unique to my clients, with the exception of the people that were actually involved. Over and over these situations play themselves out. These client experiences will give you a little peek into how people feel, engage with THE System, and encounter the higher effect of The Hire Effect.

Client Experience

> *Marie had been part of her family's business, Jacob's Kitchens and Bath, for nearly three years. Her professional background was primarily in an administrative role for her local city council. She had gotten bored with what she'd been doing for the city and came to work on the management team as support for her brother, Jake Jr., who was the CEO and primary owner.*
>
> *JKB had been in business for nearly 25 years making cabinets, and they'd employed 15 people for the last 10. Her brother asked her to be part of the interviewing process for their next hire, a customer account rep. He explained to Marie that they really wanted to grow the business, but people just weren't interested in working hard anymore. He'd hire people and, within a few short months or perhaps a year, they'd move on.*
>
> *Marie's first interview working with Jake Jr. was of a friend of his oldest son. Marie had collected nearly 15 candidates applying for the job and Patrick was the first to come in to interview. Marie and Jake Jr. sat across from Patrick, while Jake asked a few questions. Within twenty minutes, Jake appeared ready to conclude the interview.*

Marie was terribly surprised by what happened next. Jake Jr. offered him a job on the spot! Jake Jr. smiled at her after Patrick agreed to start on Thursday and said, "Well, that wasn't as bad as the last one. I had to interview four people! Let's get moving on that proposal for the Baker's."

Afterward, Marie asked a ton of questions: "Why did you pick him? He's not the most qualified. How did you choose him without even considering the others? He was 10 minutes late!"

It was clear to Marie what was wrong with the hiring—no process, no time investment, nepotism (which worked out for her when her brother offered her the job but this was ridiculous), and so much more.

Enlightened Leaders

If you do *not* see yourself in the following couple pages, it is highly unlikely you will maximize THE concepts, processes, and tools the rest of the book presents. You can save yourself some time and energy when you are done with this section if you don't truly see yourself as an ***Enlightened Leader***.

What is an Enlightened Leader?

An Enlightened Leader:

- gathers others together and truly empowers them to build a great business,
- is never done evolving herself—finding new ways to look at life and business,
- encourages professional growth for each of her team members,
- commits to process for consistent results and evolves the process to get better results, and
- holds herself responsible and accountable to reach goals

You are gathering and empowering a team to build a great business. A critical part of implementing THE is getting help doing it. Traditional western thought and culture push us to "not bother people" or "be brave and do it alone." The first traditional message, not bothering people, drives you to be nice; don't get me started on how wrong this is. The second message, do it alone, encourages you to attempt to appear impressive for achieving it alone. You and those you involve in this process will be far more effective as a unit and you won't burn yourself out along the way. Don't listen to traditional thought here. Get the help and use it.

In addition, involving others in this process can achieve powerful results. You have the benefit of seeing candidates from multiple viewpoints, your team is building relationships with the new hire the minute they walk in the door as a candidate, your team is learning valuable skills, and your time is freed up to do the things you are brilliant at. You'll hear more about THE Unconventional Hiring Team later on: how to choose them and how they can coordinate for maximum results and exponential benefits.

You are always on the search for new insights, studying other disciplines and finding ways your business can mimic the brilliance in those disciplines. You are hungry for new ways to look at life and your business. Because it's hard to predict when insights for your business will arise, it's always on your mind.

You are also clear that the more evolved and developed your team is, the more power you have to affect the things your business cares about. With respect to this and other parts of your business you have an abundance view—the more they grow the better for everyone. Investing in particular members of your team has them building a valuable skill they will take with them no matter where they go. This builds loyalty and strong bonds.

You are committed to a repeatable process so you can get consistent results. Working with your team, collaborating, and getting predictable results boils down to committing to the process and tracking results. Committing to process long enough to assess effectiveness requires a long-term game.

It's so easy to be drawn into the anxiety of trying to fill the position quickly and taking shortcuts in the process to get there. You know the saying "hire slow and fire fast." Committing to and managing THE with a team supports hiring slow.

Are you an Enlightened Leader?

THE Unconventional Hiring Team

Something I often hear from business owners is that they really want to include their team (give them responsibilities and have a structure for accountability), but hiring is really difficult to hand off. Recognize, though, it would be a mistake to totally divest yourself of the process. Don't just hand it off. Employ your own Unconventional Hiring Team to bring you the best candidates to choose from. Your team weeds out the candidates that don't fit and suss out the best in the pack, then you make the choice from there.

As a business owner you want your people to bring you problems with solutions, right? This is no different. In forming this team, you will be able to recoup a great deal of your time, build a stronger team and make a great hire.

In the following few pages I'll describe a way for you to think about forming your own hiring team and make specific requests that will result in more time for you to do what you need while still netting you better final candidates in the long run.

Before we get to hiring team formation however, a model for communication and request making I have found profoundly useful can help you and your team as well. Terry Winograd and Fernando Flores referred to this model as "the atom of trust" and "*Conversations for Action*."

In figure 1 you'll find the different speech acts that are associated with building trust over time and coordinating well. What is most important for you to glean from this model is that there are promises being made. This may feel a bit intense when you consider that some of the promises might be things like promising to send an email, add a name to a list, or update a script. What's critical here is for you to understand that the better you and your team get at coordinating around promises, the better you'll be able to work with one another to hire the best new person.

A couple quick things about this model and then we'll move on. Being a good requestor is just as important as being a good promisor. A good request always contains the following: a very clear description of what you want and a time/date you want it by. Satisfaction only comes when the requestor gets what he wants when he wants it.

From 1 to 3 will sound something like this:

> You: Bill, will you please get me the sales report for the quarter, and include the stats for the marketing campaign we just completed, by 9 a.m. on Friday? I need to include it in my summary report to the board before our meeting at noon that day.
>
> Bill: Absolutely.

If Bill delivers, that is a trust building experience.

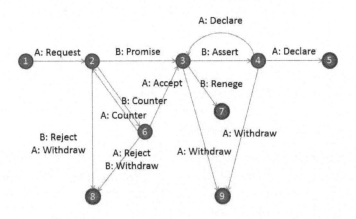

Figure 1 Conversations for Action

However, notice the speech act between 3 and 7, renege. If Bill comes to you at 8:30 on Friday morning and says he just didn't have time, the degradation of trust happens. He's reneged on his promise to you, leaving you reneging on the board, unless you can pull a rabbit out of a hat.

This model represents all the ways a conversation could go. If you take the time to get on the same page using Conversations for Action with your team, efficient and clear communications will add to your ability to coordinate with one another, whether you are hiring or coordinating for any number of reasons.

In addition, making promises to candidates and delivering on them will lead to a higher rate of landing a good employee. All right, let's move on. Who should you have on your hiring team?

Roles on Your Hiring Team

The following is a sketch of the roles and personalities you'll want on your hiring team. You'll want someone who:

- Is the **Decider**
- **Embodies the Culture** of your company well
- Is a good **project manager**
- Is **managing** the new hire
- Will be **a peer** of the new hire
- Is **intuitive** about people
- Has **a vested interest** in you, **knows your company** well, and could provide **great outside perspective**
    - o Investors
    - o Advisors
    - o Customers
    - o Peer Business Owners

If you have a very small team, or indeed are looking to make your first hire, I strongly encourage you to include those around you that know you and are invested in your success. Don't be a lone ranger. The results could be disastrous.

Let's take a closer look at each of the roles on your Unconventional Hiring Team.

The Unconventional Hiring Team as a Whole

Efficient coordination on the team will reinforce and produce many things, including the following:

- **A culture** you want
- **Good working relationships** between team members
- **A foundation for the new employee** to begin their work
- **A better hire than you ever could have done on your own**
- **An outgoing message** that prospective new employees will encounter reflecting your business culture allowing you to attract a good fit

The Decider

This individual is generally either the business owner or on the executive team. One of the powerful things about having multiple individuals on the hiring team, making assessments of each of the candidates, is that they do and should have different perspectives. The Decider's role here is to make sure that the choice is good for the business. The Decider will be considering aspects of the new hire such as:

- Do we need to pay top dollar for an individual to join the team when we can gain equivalent amounts and quality of work by hiring a less impressive, perhaps less qualified candidate and shifting responsibilities to a colleague for the more high level tasks? This is holding the fiduciary role.

- Do we take into consideration some of the bonus qualities of a candidate that we hadn't considered, but will improve the possibilities of achieving the vision of our company in a more effective but different way? This is holding the visionary role.

Client Experience

> *Paul, like many company owners, was nervous about empowering his team to bring him the best candidates. From the day he started the business, he'd had hands on the entire hiring process.*
>
> *Now with THE System in place his team was empowered to bring him the top three candidates from a pool of 82 potential new employees. Prior to the final panel interviews for their new marketing director, the team that had interviewed the top three came in and gave a brief on their assessments of the candidates and how well they fit what the company wanted.*
>
> *After the three panel interviews and reviewing the assignments that they'd turned in, Paul talked through the whole panel's take on which one to hire. It was pretty clear to Paul that he had a hard choice to make—every candidate had amazing qualities. There wasn't a bad choice in the whole group from his point of view.*
>
> *Paul discovered that he was far more effective of a business leader when he asked his team to be responsible and then held them accountable. He's made 13 hires since then and each time in his role as decider—not taking on all the roles of hiring project manager, interviewer, communicator, designer AND decider.*

The Team Member That Embodies the Culture

This person ensures company culture is being deeply considered. If you've chosen well, this person really doesn't have to do much but be a good observer—they live and breathe the vision and culture of the company. When they live and breathe the culture, their commitment to protecting it will be almost pathological. This person will consider the impact of the potential hire on existing employees and future goals. They will hold questions such as the following:

- Will this person act in a way that is consistent with what we care about?
- Will this person make a positive addition to an already amazing team and culture?

Project Manager

An excellent place for most companies to get better at hiring is managing communications with prospective employees and coordinating the scheduling and information needs of the others on the team. This person will have an excellent grasp on how THE tools are used and handled.

THE Proof tools will help with the communications tracking immensely. A simple snapshot of where you are in the process—how many people are still in the running, what stage of the process they are in and what's been said to them so far—will provide a better ability to choose the right team member. Take a look at the Campaign Status Document in appendix A.

> A large part of being able to attract great people is having a reputation for treating people well. It's stressful applying and interviewing for jobs. Whatever you can do to take care of the concerns of those people, even the ones you don't end up hiring, will only make your reputation better.

Additionally, the project manager should be exceptional at being a requestor and a promisor. If they promise a candidate to get back to them by a certain date or time and they don't, that could result in the loss of a possible good hire.

The New Employee's Manager

There are two reasons including the manager in the hiring process makes a great deal of sense: it starts building the relationship before the person is brought on board, and the manager will have a very different perspective from the others on your hiring team. They will consider the following questions:

- What work will it take to manage this candidate?
- What work will it take to bring this candidate on board and have them be productive?

Giving this manager a say in who is hired will keep her engaged and will help set realistic expectations for the new hire of what their job will be like. Even if the manager doesn't get their candidate of choice, their inclusion and understanding of the rationale behind the chosen candidate will reduce the likelihood of conflict later on.

A Peer of the New Employee
If for no other reason than to see the dynamics between the peer and the candidate, this is a good inclusion. There are many other reasons you want to include this individual in the hiring team: relationship building from the get go with whomever you choose, a perspective that supports the manager in terms of how much work it will be to onboard a candidate, technical assessments of candidates skills, incentive to make a new employee successful, professional development if you see a future of management for this person in the future, and an opportunity to show off to good candidates the good people they'll be working with.

An Intuitive Person
We all know these people, the ones that can spot a good fit immediately. Intuitive people come in all shapes and sizes and all levels of an ability to say why a person fits or not. Later on you'll see more about THE Proof tools, which will temper or manage the intuitive people that often can't say why a person is a good fit or not.

This is not obvious and can be nerve wracking to implement when the first person that comes to mind has no connection at all to your hiring process or the group the new candidate would be working in, or has a low level of responsibility within the company.

It doesn't matter if the intuitive is the COO, a social media associate, or a truck driver. This intuitive could be incredibly helpful in spotting THE Right Fit or, indeed, the wrong fit.

Client Experience

> *John immediately thought of an intuitive he wanted on the team but it just seemed too outside the realm of "normal" for him. Well, this isn't normal thinking, so I advised John to get over it.*
>
> *The intuitive, Shiela, was a caterer for John's monthly community lunches. Shiela was very approachable; we talked with her about our appreciation for her way with people and explained that her role in John's hiring team would be in the last panel interviews. She would get a little 30 minute training on how to use the tools she'd need to work with the rest of the team and we promised she'd learn something about hiring for herself if she participated occasionally.*
>
> *During the panel interview of the top three candidates for VP of Sales, Shiela provided observations and assessments of each candidate that were invaluable to John. She spotted attributes and connections that made it clear who fit into John's culture and could meet the needs of the role.*

An Individual with Vested Interest

Perhaps the least obvious people to include on a hiring team are those **outside** your company. Think about people who you know well and vice versa. They can provide a perspective you couldn't possibly get from within your company.

Two things about the choosing of these people you should consider:

- You can use these people strategically in the hiring process and can, but don't have to, train them completely on THE System to get a powerful return on the value they will bring by being involved.

- If you are making your first hire, this is the only option you have if you don't want to do this alone, and you shouldn't. You don't need to be a lone ranger when you are hiring, whether it's your 100th employee or your first.

Client Experience

> *One of the very first clients of THE in 2009 was looking for a business partner to join her. Melissa had launched two years prior and had five contractors working with her. She was about to take on another major client, but it was clear that her company was going to have to expand. After much consideration she went on the hunt to find someone who would want to take on the risk of being a partner in her business. She shaped what she thought the partnership would look like and put the word out through her business contacts.*
>
> *Amazingly, there were four people who she'd worked with in different ways that wanted to be in conversation with Melissa about a partnership. However, two of the four owned companies that could be great to join forces with, so she moved them forward into conversation.*
>
> *She felt alone and too exposed to make the decision on her own and she found THE. After a few sessions to develop her Hiring Team, she involved someone she would never otherwise have thought to include—her first customer, Tom. Tom was a repeat customer since his first engagement and relied heavily on Melissa's company.*
>
> *After a few discussions with Tom about this, he was not only honored to be part of the process but he felt*

empowered to affect the stability of one of his most trusted vendors, Melissa!

Tom and Melissa comprised her hiring team. Using THE System they created THE Obstacle Course that the two possible partners would go through. Their work together resulted in a merging of two companies and a very happy partnership to this day.

Conclusion

As an Enlightened Leader, forming this team and truly empowering them to bring you the best candidates to choose from could be a game changer for you. It could also be a tremendous challenge if you tend to micromanage or are under a great deal of stress to get someone into a position quickly.

Try it. What you'll find is a liberty you hadn't known was possible and a structure for getting other things done you hadn't considered before.

Initial Actions

Go through the different roles on THE Unconventional Hiring Team and write down a name for each one.

Gather your hiring team in a meeting and:

- convey your investment in a process for getting better at hiring;
- let them know the benefits of being included, as well as the benefits you get from including them; and
- get their thoughts and buy in.

Adjust your hiring team after the discussion. Who was interested and committed? Who did you think would be valuable in the process?

THE Right Fit™

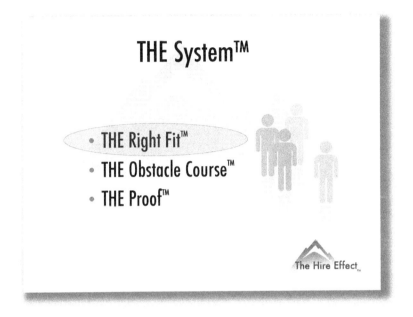

THE Right Fit™ is the first component of THE System. It is a construction of exactly what you want and need in your next employee. It's a representation of the ideal candidate. Do they fit your culture? Do they have the skills and personality traits to ensure success?

Figure 2 is a visual representation of the high level components that make up THE Right Fit—an effective model for THE Right Fit will have three *core values*, three *manner descriptors*, three skills and three traits.

Humans are decision-making, judging machines. We are constantly forming opinions: "She's so smart." "He sure knows a lot about healthcare reform." "He's not very effective at communicating." It's natural. Peter Denning refers to them as "assertions"—more about that later. Your opinions are what you use to make decisions for yourself and those around you, decisions like whom to offer a job to.

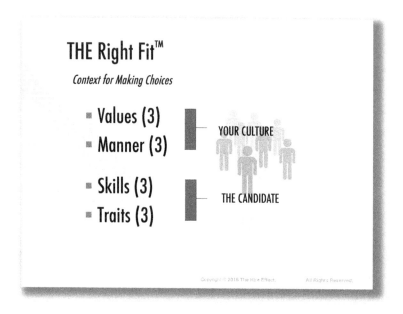

Figure 2. THE Right Fit™ is a snap shot of the perfect candidate.

You need context to make good decisions. For instance, unless you know what a room is going to be used for, you can't say that it's an effective room or not. If you were going to have a meeting that requires real creativity and constant collaboration with others resulting in a business vision for the next 5 years, choosing the basement room of the town hall with no windows, a classroom style set up, and a chilly temperature would likely be ineffective. Everyone would be cold, unable to freely work creatively, and boxed in. But if you want to meet to quickly get the team up to date on something and don't want people sticking around afterward, this might be perfect. Deciding on the right room depends upon the context of what you'll use it for.

Choosing people you'd like to make a job offer to is similar. If you want to hire a new sales lead, you'll want that person to fit snugly into your culture and have all the skills and traits of a good sales representative.

THE Right Fit is a construct of the ideal individual that includes a clear picture of your culture (core values and the manner in which work is done) and the candidate's attributes (skills and personality traits). Each one of the core values is a context point, as is each of the manners, skills and traits. In a good construct of THE Right Fit, you'll have 12–18 context points.

In figure 3, you'll see a detailed example of THE Right Fit, including the context points listed as "attributes", that a hiring team would use to orient themselves before interviewing a candidate. This represents work for a client that owns a home care agency, WeCare.com (they employ caregivers that serve their customers—the elderly and infirmed). Although the top section regarding culture will be the same for all new hires in your company, the bottom part is all about what you need in a role—this one is for the Marketing Lead at WeCare.com. Let's take a look at the different components of this example and walk through how you might figure these components out.

Your Company Culture

It is unusual for small businesses to take into consideration business culture when considering candidates for a new position. Oddly enough, this is the piece that can be the most critical.

Your articulation of your business culture takes time to construct but is relatively static, so you only have to revisit this perhaps once or twice per year with very little changes. An important point here is that you want the culture to reflect your company *as it is*, not as you want it. If you aren't happy with what you come up with as a representation how your culture is now, an organizational change initiative may be in order, which will take time, intention and a great deal of focus.

THE Right Fit™

Position: *Marketing Lead*

		Attribute	Definition	What does it look like?
Company Culture - Values + Manners	Values	Caring	Exhibiting kindness and concern for others.	Asking questions about others Doing for others without asking Observant of others in surrounding
		Community	Committed to being part of something that is bigger than themselves.	Interest in others & connection Getting together in and out of work Enlisting others in action/cause
		Beyond	Not just meeting expectations. Doing what is not necessarily expected and is appreciated.	Answering questions but more fully than expected Doing what is assigned and giving a little extra
	Manners	Willing	Ready and eager to take on challenges and tasks	Complying to requests without hesitation A happy disposition when asked to do something regardless of the task
		Flexible	Capable of shifting or modifying processes, behaviors, thinking to accommodate for the greater good.	Willing to examine a different way of doing things Not set on having things a certain way Accepting that a process they are used to can be changed.
		Supportive	Providing encouragement, emotional or practical help that allows others to succeed or be more comfortable	Making an offer to help Vocal and body language showing empathy for others
Candidate	Skills	Strong Relationship Building	Exhibits a wide range of individuals in their network that are willing to assist or expand capacity to get new customer prospects	Has many referrences to call upon for employment Can easily call upon old colleagues or friends to assist in getting oriented in a new position or project
		Clear Communication	Able to speak and write in a clear and compelling manner	Can speak clearly and get key messages across without difficulty Can write clearly and get key messages across without grammatical errors
		CRM capable	Skilled in a customer relations management tool and can exhibit ability to keep track of prospects	Is knowledgable about tools such as Sales Force or Sugar Shows good organizational skills around different stages of marketing prospects
		Self Starter	Consistently accomplishes goals and completes projects with little or no direction	Suprising results - past expectations Seeks to fully understand and execute on projects
	Traits	Inclusive	Works well with others and considers others goals and interests	Invites others to participate Shows interest in opinions of others Discusses and creates new solutions with others
		Friendly	Provides a welcoming and easeful atmosphere to those they encounter	smiles readily curious quick to compliment and include

Rev - 111616   Copyright(C)TheHireEffect 2015

Figure 3. Example of THE Right Fit™.

Core Values

Few small businesses have core values that are identified, embodied by their teams, *and* embedded in processes like: hiring, selling, marketing, performance assessments, and visioning. This isn't a bad thing; it's just a great opportunity for improvement.

If you don't have core values identified, there's no need to spend more than a few hours with the right people (see Initial Actions at the end of this chapter for more on this group of people), constructing and agreeing on what is an important set of core values.

> *Core values* are principles, ethics and/or deeply held beliefs.

Any more than four or five core values can reduce the effectiveness of having them in the first place. In THE Certification (appendix C), we bring the identified hiring team and the leadership team together, and work through a facilitated process to be certain the culture is crisply and appropriately identified.

What is most important is to identify a set of words or phrases that exemplify your company principles and deeply held beliefs, then get everyone on the same page.

I'm not sure if you caught that so I'll say it again—get everyone on the same page. The discussion that leads to the identified core values can be as important as the resultant words. Earlier I mentioned that business is in language and this is a clear example of that. Aside from how we coordinate getting things done (remember Conversations for Action), it is much more likely we will have an outcome we want when we are using the same language.

Imagine this team of people working together: Jacque, a native French speaker; Pedro, a native Spanish speaker; Helen a native Dutch speaker; and Franklin a native English speaker. If none speak the others' language, they've not a chance of getting much done quickly or much done at all.

Now imagine a team that all happen to speak English as a native language, but each member was raised by parents with these different backgrounds: career military, surfing pros, neuropsychologists, and politicians. Coordinating so that everyone is "on time" might be a bit of a challenge. Typically teams like this will eventually learn what each means by "on time," but not until after many instances of the military brat sitting and waiting—"on time" to them means at least 15 minutes early, while arrival within 20 to 30 minutes of the agreed time is "on time" to the team member raised by the surfing pros.

Now what does that mean to you with respect to your core values? Choose a word or phrase you think could be a core value and ask the next five people you meet what it means to them. Their responses might be close, but they'll all be slightly different. Again, the important thing is for you all to be on the same page about what your core values mean and what it looks like for someone to embody them.

Client Experience

> *Jake, owner and operator of a product design firm, was pretty certain he knew what the core values of his company were:* **expedient, flexible,** *and* **elegant***. He was pretty sure of this even though they'd never formally incorporated these or any other core values into their marketing, visioning, or everyday discussions.*
>
> *THE Unconventional Hiring Team Jake formed gathered along with the rest of his leadership team (eleven total) and ran through an exercise in which each individual independently produced three words that they thought represented the company's core principles and deeply held beliefs. Jake, of course, was part of this as well.*

The resulting list:

Fast (5)	*Caring*	*Elegant*
Organized (3)	*No more, no less*	*Flexible*
Clear (3)	*Forthright*	*Unique*
Collaborative (2)	*Truthful*	*Quick*
Speedy (2)	*No nonsense*	*Respectful*
Focused (2)	*Intent*	
Specialized	*Expedient*	

After a 30 minute facilitated discussion, the team ended up with these three core values: Fast, Focus and Custom. At one point, the project manager on the hiring team remarked, "Isn't it amazing how words like flexible, custom, and specialized mean nearly the same thing? We just needed to say what we meant out loud, and suddenly we were all in agreement."

Just three weeks after this work was done, Jake gave his normal first Monday standup with all 75 of his employees. When he asked what was the most valuable thing the company had done in the past month, one of the engineers shouted out, "The Core Values! Now we know who we are!" They were the same people as before; they were just all speaking the same language.

Back to figure 3. If you and your team have a shared story of what your core values are, what they mean and what it looks like for someone to hold them as their own, you'll all be better able to recognize THE Right Fit when he or she walks in the door!

Manner

The second component of your company's culture is the manner in which the work is done. For many years I have referred to this component as the Mood of the team. This is talked about a great deal in companies as observations from customers, vendors, and even team members: "Wow, everyone here is so friendly." or "I know I'll get it straight as an arrow from your people. They are always focused on being clear and up front with me." or "Have you noticed how our team really geeks out when they talk about our products? It's so fun to listen to."

As with core values, identifying three to five descriptors of the manner of work in your company can have a profound effect on what choice you make from the candidate pool next. In figure 3 the manner descriptors of the example home care agency are Willing, Flexible, and Supportive.

Close your eyes and imagine walking into your office or having a team meeting. What does it feel like? Can you pick a few descriptors without even trying? I bet you can.

In the next chapter we'll be talking a lot about how to figure out if a candidate might fit with respect to the manner in which work is done on a daily basis in your company. The main tool you'll be using is an *assignment*. But first we need your whole team on the same page again; how is work done in your company, what words would you use to describe the mood, and what behaviors can you "see" and "feel" that fit?

This might be a little uncomfortable at first. THE Microsoft tools include an exercise to identify the manner descriptors. For manner, we apply something similar to the process we use for core values. Getting close is what you want. This isn't a precise process and you can shift your articulation of your culture (through the manner descriptors you use).

Have everyone work separately to write down five to seven words that they feel are appropriate descriptors of the manner in which your work is done. These words are adjectives like cheery, messy, somber, organized, elegant, precise, or hectic. Clearly, there are hundreds of adjectives you can use.

Once each team member responds and all the descriptors are listed together, there will likely be overlap. Through a process of elimination the team can choose three to five of them as the manner descriptors. Again, THE Microsoft tools include this exercise in detail.

Ideally you'll want descriptors that are the way work is being done, not the way you *aspire* for it to be done. See more about this in the example section about messy.

Client Experience

Mike had owned and run his publishing business for more than 20 years and he was third generation too. He loved his company and was pretty clear they needed to hire thinking of their culture. He and his predecessors had defined core values starting from day one of the publishing house. What was new for Mike and his leadership team was thinking of culture with the inclusion of "how" they did the work.

Mike, like other THE clients, participated in a facilitated discussion to identify just how to talk about the Mood of their company. In short, they were looking to bring to light the manner descriptors they would use to round out the components of THE Right Fit as it pertained to culture.

After 45 minutes of discussion with the leadership team and the hiring team combined, three words were circled on the white board at the head of the room: quick paced, humble and messy.

Mike had made a commitment during the process not to lead to the identification of the words but to participate like everyone else. The moment the word messy was circled and agreed upon he stood swiftly and slapped the table in an uncharacteristic show of irritation. "That can't be! I will not have us known as messy!"

After a short break the whole group discussed "messy" further and felt pretty strongly about it. There, an initiative to change that part of the culture of the company was born. Although they used messy as a context point, they brought this up in deliberate discussion with the final candidates for Chief of Operations. It became a regular part of discussions and a starting point for new habits for everyone. Although it took more than 9 months, Mike and the leadership team felt like they'd made it.

What Mike was particularly thankful for in THE process of identifying his company's culture was that the process itself clearly identified something he'd always wanted to change and now he had 14 people as committed to he was to do just that.

Candidate Skills and Traits

You've heard of trying to put a square peg into a round hole. You've probably even tried to pound a square peg or two in yourself. The analogy sets you up to be looking for the shape hole you have so you can find the peg you need.

If you play out this concept and you are talking about a team of complex human beings, the pegs (the skills and personality traits you need) start to look like this:

To figure out what the hole looks like, you'll need to know what you already have on your team. Generally, CEOs and Presidents intuitively know what is needed. If that's the case, you can forge ahead.

If you aren't sure what skills and traits you do need, or you are clear it's a great time to shift the team around a bit, you'll want to look at the section Consideration | THE Team Assessment in the last chapter of the book.

Skills

Once you have identified the role your new employee will be playing, you'll be able to more quickly identify the key skills you need to add to THE Right Fit for your open position. My experience is that the "role" is traditionally constructed as a listing of tasks, as opposed to a clear statement of the areas of responsibility an employee agrees to be held accountable for.

Answering the question, "What areas of the business will this new employee be accountable for?" will be more powerful as you bring this new team member on board.

> Think of a *role* as a high level view, or agreement, of the areas of responsibility a person holds or will hold as your new employee.

If a listing of tasks describes the work for a new employee, there will be a great deal of room for miscommunication about who is accountable for what. In addition if you are thinking of filling a position with a listing of tasks as your guideline for the skills you want, you'll be filling that position with an incomplete picture of what you actually need.

Picture yourself on a cherry picker at ground level. All you can see are those that immediately surround you and the things they are doing at the moment. With a boost about 2 stories up, you'll quickly see the layered view of all your employees working to put what you do together. It's a complicated set of processes and communication.

You'll see the person you just spent a bit of time on ground level with, but how they move about and work with different people or departments in your company. What is it that they do from day to day, week to week, and so on, that they are accountable for? How would you describe their bigger body of work?

The point here is that instead of having a comprehensive list of things that people do or will be doing, you have each holding an area of responsibility. We'll discuss more about figuring out what responsibilities you actually need someone taking up in the last chapter.

Let's look at figure 3 again in the case of the home care agency Marketing Lead. These skills listed in THE Right Fit were brought forth from the understanding that the Marketing Lead's responsibility was to create new customer acquisition.

The example home care agency structured their skill context as: Strong Relationship Building, Clear Communication, and CRM Capable. Yours may be different based on who you have on the team and what other responsibilities you'd like the candidate to hold.

The set of key skills you want to use in THE Right Fit, just like the other three groups in THE Right Fit, can have more than three items—just remember to construct THE Right Fit so that it is doable. You want to have an effective process to assess the skills you need, so choose a small number but make them the key or critical skills the candidate must have.

Sometimes this listing of skills can be incomplete or inappropriate. If you aren't sure in the design of the role what skills are necessary, a little research is in order. You may want to ask yourself: What skills were lacking in the last marketing lead? What skills clearly align with getting quarterly goals met?

Work with the hiring team to bring the key skills into THE Right Fit. When you reach THE Obstacle Course and you are looking at the kinds of assignments you want candidates to complete, you may want to tweak THE Right Fit skills a bit: add a skill, slightly change a skill, and the like.

Traits

"We need someone who is a great listener." or "We need an optimist in here ASAP. We stink!" These two statements represent the two ways you'll want to think when constructing the personality traits of THE Right Fit.

If you are mindful of what traits don't already exist on your team AND mindful of what personality traits will be most successful in the role you've specified, there's a greater likelihood of success and efficiency.

Candidate	Supportive	Providing encouragement, emotional or practical help that allows others to succeed or be more comfortable	Making an offer to help. Vocal and body language showing empathy for others
Skills	Written Communication	Capable of constructing well thought out and compelling marketing communication pieces	Can write clearly and get key messages across without grammatical errors. Emails are clean, understandable and professional
Skills	Familiar w/Visual Design Tools	Has a basic understanding of visual design tools.	Exceptionally examples are results and what software they've used. Can site several steps in using Adobe Acrobat editor
Skills	Goal Oriented	Deadline conscious, self-starter, proactive, etc.	Can explain clearly and completely how they invent goals. Exhibits knowledge of communication processes that keep management in the loop on progress being made
Traits	Social	Ability to relate in an easeful way with other people.	Can easefully participate in small talk. Initiates conversation and engages with even shy people well
Traits	Passionate	Excited to be working on obtaining new customers.	Lights up when asked about work projects. Has stories about success and excited about them
Traits	Focused	Staying in the work of marketing and understands how it fits into the big picture.	Answers questions completely even multipart questions. Clearly understands the area of expertise and doesn't offer judgement for areas outside of their own

Figure 4. An example of THE Right Fit for the candidate side.

There is compelling evidence that a diverse team is a productive and efficient one. There are many examples of this. In a recent Harvard Business Review Article "Diverse Teams Feel Less Comfortable — and That's Why They Perform Better," authors Rock, Grant and Gray highlight that with diverse teams better results are effected when team mates consciously taking one another's perspectives.

Figure 4 is an example of THE Right Fit traits that were developed using a combination of both approaches to identifying traits. The skills and traits were specifically for a customer care representative that would also be assisting the internal marketing team.

At first this may seem awkward and you may want to make sure that you have the exact right traits. The truth is there is no wrong answer here. You will get better at assessing what personality traits are best as you use THE Right Fit tool. Ideally you will want to start with something and test it out. Can you spot the personality traits you want in other team members? What were they doing that made you think they had those traits?

Conclusion
We've all experienced jigsaw puzzles. If you don't know the shape and characteristics of the piece you are looking for, you'll have to try each and every piece that is still unattached.

THE Right Fit can be a powerful tool if you let it. Just knowing what your culture is and saying it out loud works wonders. You can reinforce this by bringing culture to the forefront in processes like performance reviews; quarterly status meetings; or new process flows for sales, marketing, product development, and the like. Additional thoughts on Seating Your Culture will be discussed in the last chapter.

Initial Actions

Having a crisp articulation of your company culture is incredibly valuable to you and getting a crisp articulation can be easier than you might think.

First, you'll need to identify the people who should be part of this exercise: those on your leadership team and those on THE Unconventional Hiring Team. Use the term "leadership team" loosely. When in doubt about including someone, just include her. You should remember, though, that you already have a culture, and this exercise is simply revealing it. When you complete this exercise, those that know your company well should all be nodding their heads and smiling in agreement.

Depending upon the size of your company, I'd guess there could be anywhere from three to 15 people in the room. You'll need about two hours.

1. Read the definition of a core value.

2. Ask each individual to write down without discussion with others the three words or short phrases that they feel represent the core values of your company.

3. As a group, put all the core values on a screen or board for everyone to see.

4. As a group, collect all the similar words like speedy, quick, fast, and expedient into one group.

5. Identify as a group the top three to five words.

6. With each core value agree upon a collective definition of what each of those words means.

7. Repeat this process for the manner descriptions.

THE Obstacle Course

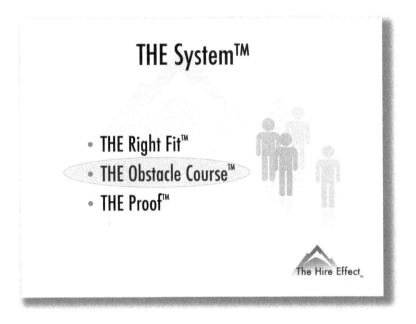

Now that you know what you are looking for, you're on to the next step, designing an obstacle course for the candidates.

The Obstacle Course incorporates two different levels of engagement of your hiring team, **low-touch** and **high-touch steps**, and one critical component at every step that gets your candidates to reveal their true behavior, *assignments*.

Years ago (beginning in the '70s), hiring managers and departments made a transition in the recruiting world to something called "behavioral interviewing." The premise of behavioral interviewing is that a great predictor of a person's future performance is past performance. So the questions you ask that are based on behavior interviewing techniques are the ones getting the candidate to recall a time when . . .

A great example that comes up often in hiring is testing for the ability to handle stress. How in the world do you determine if a person handles stress well? According to RecruitLoop, an online recruiting company, questions like the following are useful:

- What has been the most stressful situation you have ever found yourself in at work? How did you handle it?
- What have you done in the past to prevent a situation from becoming too stressful for you or your colleagues to handle?

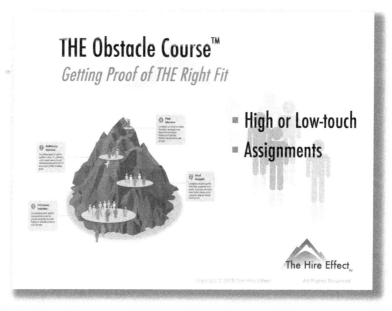

Katharine Hansen, PhD, of Quintessential CareersBlog, suggests that asking behavioral interviewing questions gets you to about 55% of predictive behavior. This is a huge improvement from non-behavioral interviewing techniques. With THE System and the use of assignments, we incorporate as a key factor in creating the obstacle course something I like to call "experiential interviewing."

Client Experience

> Tim, a business owner of a software company, was very dedicated to pair programming. In the later part of THE Obstacle Course for his developer role, he would have a specific problem to be solved through a few new lines of code. He would have the hopeful candidate sit with one of his current developers and ask them to work together to write the code. This exercise generally took about 30–45 minutes. It was quite often evident through this assignment whether a candidate had done pair programming and actually preferred working that way, and who hadn't and didn't.
>
> An additional significant revelation for Tim during these exercises was whether the candidate would step up and take the lead in the programming or sit back and allow their temporary partner to do everything.
>
> This simple assignment often saved Tim from having to do a panel interview, which is very high touch for his hiring team.

The last component of THE Obstacle Course design that can make or break your process is the number of steps you include. Let's walk through the components separately.

Low Touch and High Touch

Many who have interviewed know that they need to cull the candidate pool in the beginning to save a bit of time on the back end of the hiring process. Why spend time on interviewing a candidate that doesn't have the base qualifications you need? Being clear on whether a step is low touch or high

> **Low-touch steps** will be low impact on your hiring team's time and quickly identify those candidates that clearly aren't a match for THE Right Fit.

touch will help the team to stay on track to make quick but proven decisions about moving candidates on to the next stage.

Low-touch steps include tactics like resume and cover letter reviews, five-minute phone screens, online questionnaires, and work sample submissions. There are many more low-touch steps that can be employed here. The better you and your team get at inventing and employing the low-touch steps, the more time you'll save processing candidates that clearly didn't fit in the beginning.

A few things about low-touch steps that touch back on THE Right Fit and forward (the next chapter in fact) on THE Proof. The low-touch steps are really meant to clearly identify those that won't fit, not necessarily to identify and move on the one's that do. The key here is to orient yourself and your team on getting clear proof that someone doesn't fit. THE Obstacle Course you use which will include high-touch steps will take care of proving the candidates that remain DO fit.

> ***High-touch steps*** will take more of you and your team's time and, with that investment of time, will build the proof you need for the best match possible for THE Right Fit.

Not to beat a dead horse, but this point has to be clear for the process to be effective. With low-touch steps you'll be using the context of THE Right Fit to release the ones that don't fit.

An example here might be helpful. Using the bulleted skills and traits below as part of THE Right Fit, you may decide to continue with a candidate whose response to your phone screen had you questioning if they really were familiar with Visual Design Tools. However, you would release the candidate that proved their written communication skills were NOT good.

Skills
- Good Written Communications
- Familiar w/Visual Design Tools
- Goal Oriented

Traits
- Social
- Passionate
- Focused

You are working with these steps to take out of the candidate pool those that absolutely won't work.

High-touch steps include tactics like one-on-one interviews, panel interviews, team introductions, board introductions, and the like. The better you and your team get at inventing and employing the high-touch steps, the more effective you'll be able to spot components of onboarding plans, make effective use of you and your team's time, and indeed, choose THE Right Fit.

Working on the premise that a high-touch step is meant to make good use of the time you are investing by finding the proof, these steps need to be highly coordinated by and among the hiring team members. Each member will make their own observations so the design of this part of THE Obstacle Course will need to reveal authentic behavior—behavior of the candidate that is likely to be how they act normally.

This is "experiential interviewing"—matching how candidates act and listening to what they say. If you have designed a good obstacle course, you will be observing candidates closely and comparing them to THE Right Fit, this is the magic of The Hire Effect.

Assignments

The design of THE Obstacle Course, as mentioned earlier, includes **assignments**. Most small business owners and operators are very familiar with assignments as they pertain to

> An *assignment* is anything you ask the candidate to do for you in the interview process.

the low-touch steps. They gather resumes and sort them from high to low for qualifications. They have candidates write cover letters to see what they would like to highlight about themselves. They have them fill out applications.

What small business owners and operators aren't very familiar with is continuing the use of assignments into the later parts of the interview process. This is a missed opportunity to observe yet more behavior that will help you make a good choice. Key to designing a good assignment into each step is to keep in mind what THE Right Fit looks like and how you might get the candidate to reveal behavior that is in keeping with that or not.

You'll want to include four things in each assignment request:
- a clear description of what the assignment is,
- a specific date and time to complete the assignment, and
- to whom you want them to deliver the assignment.

Let's stop and think for a moment about the skill that many job seekers have—they're what we call in the industry a "good interviewer." They are capable of putting their good foot forward at every step of a short interview process.

Good interviewers can be very compelling to small business owners that really need to hire quickly. Your intuition is telling you that this is the right person for the job. You should make a move now so you don't lose them. It would make things so easy to hire them now.

With persistence and a strong commitment to have each candidate go through THE Obstacle Course, you and your hiring team will have the ability to spot the inevitable appearance of weaknesses in the good interviewer, which will be invaluable to your business in the long run. Hiring slow isn't always an easy thing to do, but sticking to THE Obstacle Course will help.

Client Experience

Melissa, a business owner of a marketing image consulting company, needed to step away from the direct sales role she was playing in her company. There were many reasons for this, but the most important to her was that she wanted her company to be able to continue and thrive without her presence.

With THE Obstacle Course she and her hiring team designed, the last step of five was for the top three candidates to participate in a panel interview. The assignment she'd given to each of them was to be prepared at this final panel interview to present a 90-Day Ramp-Up Plan. This was a first hire for her and her team with THE System, so I was deeply involved in making sure they identified a good assignment and then got the most data they could on the behavior of each of the final candidates.

As it turned out, one of the three final candidates came with a sheet of legal paper with notes from top to bottom. And we'd seen him scribbling his notes in the lobby as we were gathering the panel in the conference room. This was incredibly telling. He was preparing at the last moment for what we'd hoped was a very important opportunity to prove himself.

Melissa and the hiring team were not impressed. One of the team asked the candidate how long it took him to prepare for this meeting. His response, again, was very telling. He said it took him about five minutes and the resulting presentation showed it. There were great inconsistencies in his story about what would happen in 90 days; he had nothing to show us; and he stumbled through the presentation, looking at his notes to get through the awkward moments.

Fantastically, the other two finalists came with PowerPoint slides that were not only excellent takeaways for us but told us: what they thought they needed from Melissa and her team to be successful, what they knew about the consulting firm, and how well they knew the firm's target client. They gave Melissa an excellent plan to ramp up in 90 days no matter whom she and her team chose.

You'll hear more about how Melissa and her team chose between them in the chapter on THE Proof, but you can see that there is no end to the assignments you can design. What you choose to use as an assignment is only limited by you and your hiring team's imagination.

Other Considerations and Supporting Documents of THE Obstacle Course

With each new hiring campaign, THE Obstacle Course will require team coordination and candidate communication. On the following two pages, you'll see an example based again on the Marketing Lead for the home care agency.

As we go through figure 5, you'll see each piece in THE Obstacle Course and how it can be far more effective and efficient if they are all in place ahead of the launch of a campaign.

Supporting Document | THE Obstacle Course Graphic

The graphic of THE Obstacle Course will, at a glance, provide everyone with a good sense of where and when they are in the process. This is helpful when a candidate and hiring team communicates. Once the system is practiced and familiar to the hiring team, it represents the well-oiled machine you'll need to process candidates quickly.

Many business owners feel the pain of a tight market for talent. This is one of your best tools for having an edge on the competition for great talent. Design THE Obstacle Course and get good at it, and you'll be able to work candidates through the process quickly, be proactive, and still make a good hire.

When the market is tight and you don't have a system, you are being reactive. The talent has the power in the situation. It's too easy to be taken over by the candidate's needs and not be able to truly see if they fit your culture and your needs. Your process needs to be a well-oiled machine. You can take the power back and make offers where they make sense (and do this quickly).

Your ability to process candidates quickly and to make a good choice is critical to your business success; having that process be second nature to your hiring team in a talent-constrained market may make or break your business.

Consideration | Assignments on Site and Necessity
Wherever possible, coordinate assignments so they are done in your office or in the environment where the candidate will be working regularly. Doing this can get you a good idea of whether the candidate can produce acceptable results while experiencing a normal office experience.

For instance, if you are expecting the new employee to work in a bullpen and they have to write content, one of your assignments should be clearly designed to have them write in the bullpen on a normal day.

Secondly, if you are conducting an interview and then requesting the candidate to write in the bullpen, or whatever the assignment may be, make the determination on moving the candidate forward before having them do the assignment. There's no need for you to take up your time, or theirs, if you know they won't be moving forward in the process.

Supporting Document | Candidate Pool Tracking
Tracking your candidates can be a challenge, but, with another of THE tools, the project manager should be able to provide a pretty quick picture of how many candidates are in the pipeline and what stage each of them is currently in.

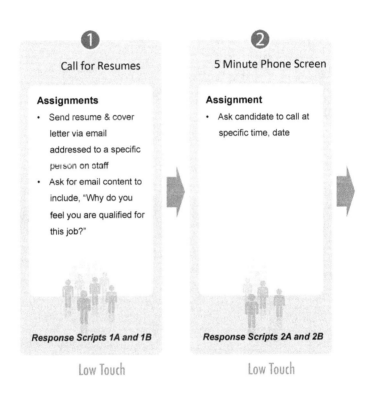

Figure 5. Example of THE Obstacle Course, page 1.

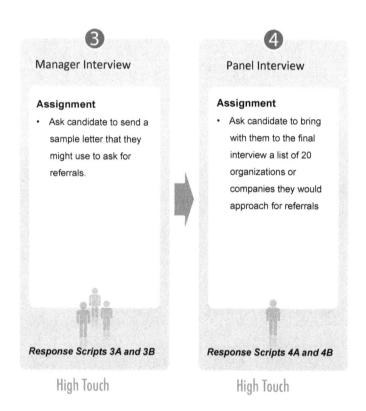

Figure 6. Example of THE Obstacle Course, page 2.

You know as a business owner how many times you have to choose to pivot or be flexible with what you spend your time on.

The power of making a clear distinction for yourself as a leader, or even as a living, acting human in the world, between *deciding* to do something and *choosing* to do something is in the opportunity cost.

As an example, let's say I decide on Saturday afternoon that we will be having tacos for dinner. Tacos sound good, right? I'm excited and pretty sure I have everything I need to make tacos in the house. Time comes to prepare the evening meal and I find that we don't have any ground beef in the house, but we do have tofu. Cool, that will make some excellent tacos I'm sure.

> *Decide*: to kill off or not consider other possibilities as you move toward your end goal.
>
> *Choose*: to consider the whole picture and, in any given moment, select a different end goal or a different tactic to reach the goal you have.

Spices are in order, but I realize I don't have any of the prepackaged taco seasoning I usually use. But hey, that's okay. I'll use red pepper flakes, ground red pepper and some chili powder. On closer inspection, I have no salsa or fresh tomatoes to make any. I'm creative. We'll just use some ketchup.

I can do this! I want tacos for dinner, dang it!

When all was said and done, we had some sort of spicy tofu ladled on top of corn chips (because we didn't have the shells either) with not nearly enough cheese. It tasted okay, but it wasn't tacos for sure. The kids turned their nose up at it: "These aren't tacos!"

Deciding on tacos took me down the path of a disappointing dinner. If I had chosen tacos, re-examined our ingredient pool, and then chosen something else, perhaps I could have come up with something far more delicious for dinner.

When you are taking a look at the candidate pool and it's not substantial enough to have a successful campaign, you can *choose* to work to find more candidates new candidates or *decide* on one that is sort of THE Right Fit. Now is the time for *choosing*. *Deciding* could cost your bottom line dearly.

Consideration | How many steps to use
The first consideration in design of the process is: just how many steps should THE Obstacle Course include in any given campaign? It will depend upon the level of complexity of the role, and, indeed, the level of importance of a good fit. Generally, THE Obstacle Course you choose should have no fewer than three steps—you'll need at least that many to suss out the good interviewer. If the flow includes more than five steps, it becomes difficult to process a candidate quickly enough before losing them to competitors. Having said that, I've seen campaigns as long as seven steps that worked incredibly well. One of those campaigns was for a new partnership role in a startup and had three low-touch steps. That ensured a quick processing time in the beginning.

Remember, each step will include an assignment so you can observe behavior. Campaigns for the general roles in a small business are most effective with four steps, two low-touch and two high-touch. There are templates to create THE Obstacle Course for three to five step processes.

In figure 5 you can see there are two low-touch steps and two high-touch steps. If you are considering a campaign for Marketing Lead of your company, this doesn't mean this is ideal for you. Much of the choice on steps will rely upon what you say the role of Marketing Lead is, who is on your hiring team, and what kind of candidate pool you have attracted.

Consideration | Strategies and Tactics for Interviewing

A good interview will get you great data for making a decision on whether to move forward with a candidate or not. Remember, your goal is NOT to have a nice conversation where you listen to candidates tell you what they think you want to hear. The goal is for you to provide ample time and opportunity for the candidates to show their true selves. This will give you plenty of proof of THE Right Fit.

Here are a few tips that will help you get what you need:

Have your Individual Candidate Tracking and Proof sheet, along with the appropriate script, in front of you, and briefly review it before the candidate arrives. Shake off the day's other duties; reviewing THE Right Fit will get you set for what you are looking for and not distracted by the million other things you feel you should be doing.

You do 10% of the talking and let them do 90% of the talking. The more they say, the more you learn about them. Start by trying to limit yourself to only asking open-ended questions. Encourage them to elaborate on their brief answers with "Anything else?," "Can you give me an example?," or "Say more about that, please." Concentrate on steering the conversation rather than dominating it. If you feel the need to put your two cents in about what the candidate is saying, try to save it for the end of the interview. If at the end you can't remember, it wasn't that important.

Insert awkward silences on occasion. No technique pulls the truth out of a candidate better than an awkward silence. It's simply human nature for the other person to start talking and fill it. Let them "feel the silence" and they will continue speaking in order to fill it. This may not be comfortable for you at first, but learning to use this technique will net you some great decision-making material for sure. When a pause in the conversation begins, just count to 3 very slowly. The classic technique of "1-Mississippi, 2-Mississippi, 3-Mississippi" works very well.

Include another interviewer that asks and says nothing. This extra pair of eyes should be on the hiring team and should also have a tracking and proof sheet with THE Right Fit context points. The purpose of the "silent interviewer" is to have someone with a different perspective. Being human, you'll each have your own take on the candidate. Also, this may sound a little sneaky, but having that person saying nothing can be unnerving and push the candidate into a more authentic behavior pattern.

Panel interviews are an excellent opportunity to coordinate as a team and get the most out of the time. Clearly, this is a high-touch step. To make the most of it, you'll need to take the time to review THE Right Fit, discuss afterward each person's observations, and be clear on the benefits/drawbacks of each candidate. Without taking that time to do all those things, the opportunity cost could be high and the value too low.

You should maintain a set of questions that you ask each candidate for a particular role. You can deep dive wherever you want with each candidate; however, having the consistency of asking the same question across the board will allow you to better compare apples to apples.

Client Experience

> *Amber, a COO for a 75-person electrical repairs shop, was in the third step of a four step Obstacle Course. This was her time to choose the three top candidates from a pool of seven. She'd brought them all in and was marching through her own interviews with them in one day. It was a long day. On THE advice, she'd invited in her administrative assistant, Jess, who was the "intuitive" on the hiring team. Jess's role was to just sit and watch.*
>
> *The role they were hiring for was a Customer Account Rep. Their business required a patient problem solver, as a great deal of their revenue relied upon repeat business. The interview was specifically designed to reveal just*

how patient and how much of a problem solver these candidates were.

Amber asked these four questions first:

- *Tell us about a time when your patience was tested on the job.*
- *If someone called the office and was immediately yelling at you, what would be the tactics you'd use to calm them?*
- *If a customer repeatedly interrupted you, what kinds of things would you say to stop the cycle?*
- *Do you have any questions for me at this point?*

As each of the seven encountered these questions, Jess was making notes regarding their body language and the ease with which they responded. He also made clear notes on the answer to the fourth question, which pointed directly to the anxiety, or lack of anxiety, that was produced by the first three questions.

Were the candidates orienting their questions around things such as what processes are in place currently to respond to these kinds of situations, what kind of authority they would have to reduce the bill, or what access the rep would have to field personnel? Or was the candidate asking questions such as "What frequency of callers are this upset?" or "Will the rep have an opportunity to do other things besides taking phone calls from customers?"

Amber and Jess were able to look at each candidate's experience and skill level regarding handling irate customers, as well as more fully look at the candidates. Although they were in agreement most of the time, there were several instances where they discussed and provided proof of skill rather than just a sense of skill. Amber is now a huge fan of panel interviewing, because she has the tools to have the discussion afterward.

Supporting Document | Assignments and Script Documents

Inside each step of figure 5, the assignment is clearly articulated with the important components of a Conversation for Action (see the first chapter on THE Unconventional Hiring Team). We'll talk more about the importance of what the candidates do in response to the assignments in the chapter on THE Proof.

For the hiring team it is important, especially in the role of project manager, to be able to access the verbiage that they'll need to use when giving the assignments. Developing the response scripts will provide consistency, allowing the project manager (or whoever will be communicating with the candidates) to cut and paste to email, as well as assuring that you are treating each candidate the same.

Passing a candidate on from Step 2 (Five Minute Phone Screen) to Step 3 (The Manager Interview) would require direction in the assignment to provide a referral letter sample and to coordinate a follow-up interview.

That Script would look something like this:

> *Dear Mr. Applicant,*
>
> *Thank you for your recent phone conversation with Janis Matten.*
>
> *We are impressed with you and would like to arrange an interview that should last about 45–60 minutes at one of these times:*
>
> *Monday at 4:30 p.m.*
> *or*
> *Tuesday at 9:30 a.m.*
>
> *You will be meeting with George Jackson, who often provides the medical assessments for our in coming customers and with whom you would be working closely should you join our team.*

Please confirm which time would work best for you by tomorrow at 5 p.m.

We are also interested in seeing a sample letter that you might use when asking for referrals from a new business contact. Please attach that letter as either a Word document or a PDF file.

Kindly,

Project Manager Jake

Or, when testing to see if a candidate has follow through, you may want to send something like this as script 1A (the message for moving on to step 2):

We were impressed with your resume and cover letter. The next step is a phone interview.

See what they do. If they respond with "Great. I'll wait to hear from you," they'll be getting script 1B (the message for not moving on to step 2) in short order. On the flip side of that, if one of the traits you are looking for is self-starter, they could answer with something like the following and most definitely move on to the next step:

Hello Jake.

It was great to get the news that the next step is a phone interview. I am available to call in at any of these times:

- *Wednesday at 8 a.m.*
- *Wednesday at 8:30 a.m.*
- *Thursday at 9:15 a.m.*
- *Thursday at 1:30 p.m.*

Please let me know which time is most convenient for your team and what number I should call.

I've attached a portfolio of my work to help you in your decision moving forward. Do you need anything else from me?

I look forward to hearing from you soon.

Mr. Candidate
555.555.5555

Consideration | Interview Script Design
Knowing what skills, traits, and culture you are looking to match makes it far easier to design a script. Generally, untrained interviewers will ask questions they think get at the skill, but rarely touch on cultural or personality aspects.

Let's dive in just a bit on a few questions that could be helpful when looking at cultural context points. Take, for example, a company that has the core values integrity, customer first, and experts; and a company mood described as listen then act, value add, and safety. A set of questions that can start to reveal coherence between candidate and company could sound something like this:

- Tell us a bit about how you build trust with your coworkers.
- When checking in with a customer to see if they are satisfied, what are some of the questions you'd ask?
- Tell us about a safety initiative you were part of.
- Tell us a bit about what drives you as a leader. What do you like about it? What don't you like about it?
- Think about what it looks like to be an expert at something, both from your own perspective and from the viewpoint of your colleagues working in different industries and companies. Describe that for us, please.

The answers to these questions or requests get the candidate talking, and you'll find those context points showing up in their language or not. Diving down into follow-up questions and using the awkward silence technique can reveal more and more.

Consideration | Campaign Timeline
Working back from the date you want to have a new hire begin will help to construct the rest of the timeline. There are many factors that could influence the new hire date you *choose* including situations where:

- the role is directly customer delivery and will impact a customer.
- the market is severely talent constrained,
- knowledge transfer needs to be complete before the departure of another employee,
- revenue goals need billing in order to achieve them, or
- you or someone else on your team will drop dead if you don't get some help.

With good planning and execution a normal hiring timeline (see appendix B for an example) is between six and eight weeks. Driving toward a deadline to hire can motivate your team in many ways. Scheduling interviews at the convenience of both your team and the candidate and building critical mass for candidates to run through THE Obstacle Course are likely to be the most difficult components of reaching your deadline to hire.

Your secret weapons to still hitting your target hire date are a referral network for talent (the last of the strategies for building a good candidate pool in the next section) and excellent coordination around Conversations for Action.

Consideration | An Observation in Listening
You and your team's ability to listen closely, think critically and design follow-up questions on the spot is key to gathering assertions you need to compare to THE Right Fit.

Challenge your team, and indeed yourself, to build listening skills by attending a meeting or having lunch with a colleague and follow these simple guidelines.

You may not speak unless:

- you are observing basic niceties such as thank you, please, you are welcome, hello and goodbye, etc.
- you are making basic listening noises or words such as "I see", "okay...", "hmm", etc.
- you have been asked a question - in which case you may only simply answer the question but no more.
- you are asking questions. Likely the conversation will be very awkward unless those questions are open ended. Ask questions that require thought and more complex answers than a simple yes or no.

When you are asked a question, fight the urge to share more. Often times an open-ended question about their question will lead you to a place in which you can provide a clear answer.

Throughout the conversation you are looking to truly understand what your colleague thinks and feels about your question.

You can see the whole exercise in Appendix D.

Consideration | Building a Good Candidate Pool

Your immediate thought is to post to Indeed, Recruiter.com, Monster, or some other matching online tool. This tactic is a great place to start, but just as diverse revenue streams help mitigate the risk of going out of business quickly when one client leaves, having a strategy for getting candidates that includes a number of tactics will better ensure they will apply when you need them to.

A good solid strategy will include at least three or four of the following tactics:

- Posting to an online matching tool (e.g., Indeed.com or Monster) appropriate for the talent you are looking for

- Encouraging employee referrals (tapping into the trust your employees have built with colleagues outside your company)
- Being connected to the community of passive talent
- Investing in an internship or training program to build the talent
- Purposeful networking by you and each of your hiring team to grow and improve referrals

The least obvious and employed of the above tactics is strategies for growing and improving referrals. The fundamentals of a strong referral network include:
- trust,
- numerous mutually beneficial relationships, and
- an intentional tracking process.

Without *trust*, efforts to grow a referral network will fall flat. Trust is the fundamental building block of devoted customers, dependable vendors, and dedicated referrers.

Trust begins and grows as promises are made and kept. As mentioned in the first chapter (THE Unconventional Hiring Team), Fernando Flores and his coauthor, Terry Winograd, invented Conversations for Action (also referred to as the atom of trust). This model helps you visualize what it takes to build trust, coordinate commitments effectively, and be conscious of promises made, accepted, and kept. Strong trust comes from multiple experiences of successful collaboration to take care of mutual concerns.

The second component of a strong referral network is *numerous mutually beneficial relationships*. "Numerous" is a rather vague term and is relative to the number of candidates you hope to gather from this source. The importance here again lies in not relying on one revenue stream, one vendor, or one referral source for talent to build your candidate pool. The other distinction to be clear on in this component is "mutually beneficial relationships." This is a shared understanding of what is important for each party. Although knowing what you each care about and need is important, it is equally important to take action on one another's behalf—demonstrate, don't just talk about a commitment to help the other party achieve their goals and visions. With action you have skin in the game, and likely the referrer has an interest in returning the favor.

The last component, *a tracking process*, is very familiar to most of you in relation to customer-relations management. CRM software like Sugar, SalesForce, or Zoho is just as effective at managing these relationships as it is at your sales pipelines. Having a good way of tracking your contacts and knowing when it's time to do coffee, make a phone call, or send an email will help to manage the actions you commit to and help to build trust for a much stronger referral network.

Consideration | Constructing a Good Job Posting
Small businesses typically don't have a good clear picture of their culture in their job postings. As mentioned earlier, once the culture articulation is in place, outward-bound messaging can start to attract talent as well as customers, strategic partners, and the like.

If the language you use to advertise or talk about the job opening reflects your culture, you will have more candidates "choosing themselves in" that are appropriate for you to be considering, as well as more inappropriate candidates "choosing themselves out," or choosing *not* to apply. That alone can provide you with a more efficient hiring practice than no process at all.

Here is a pretty a typical job posting:

Baleson. *Bringing new life to senior living.*

Your responsibilities:
- Greet visitors at the community's front reception desk in a professional and pleasant manner.
- Receive incoming calls and ensure questions and needs are directed to the appropriate person.
- Serve as community ambassador to visitors; answer general questions from potential residents and inquiring families and provide informational brochures and packets as requested.
- Perform administrative and clerical support tasks for the community, including updating resident rosters and distributing mail.

Required skills and qualifications:
- High school diploma or GED equivalent
- One year office experience
- Excellent communication and customer service skills
- Proficiency with computers and word processing software, and basic typing skills
- Flexible schedule, including availability to work evenings, weekends, and holidays as needed
- Must enjoy working with the senior population

Baleson is an EOE (Equal Opportunity Employer) and drug-free workplace.

Baleson offers a number of benefits to full-time associates including, but not limited to: medical, dental, vision, disability, life, paid time off, and educational reimbursement. All associates age 21 and older are eligible to participate in the 401(k) retirement savings plan.

Here's the same ad with a bit about the culture and Baleson uses it to their advantage.

Baleson. *Bringing new life to senior living.*

The Baleson hiring team is looking for a Receptionist here at our main office. At Baleson we exceed expectations and meet our residents' needs for a holistic community. We run a neat and tidy facility with an optimistic and proactive outlook every day. We are looking for a new team member to take responsibility for upholding these principles and making our customers happy.

Your responsibilities:
- Manage visitors' and callers' first impressions and customer satisfaction
- Provide support for the sales team by informing and welcoming potential residents
- Ensure schedules for current residents run smoothly

Required skills and qualifications:
- High school diploma or GED equivalent
- One year office experience
- Excellent communication and customer service skills
- Proficiency with computers and word processing software, and basic typing skills
- Flexible schedule, including availability to work evenings, weekends, and holidays as needed
- Must enjoy working with the senior population

Metrics for Success:
- Customer satisfaction
- Phone and Front Desk Coverage
- Attendance and Reliability

Baleson is an EOE (Equal Opportunity Employer) and drug-free workplace.

Baleson offers a number of benefits to full-time associates including, but not limited to: medical, dental, vision, disability, life, paid time off, educational reimbursement. All associates age 21 and older are eligible to participate in the 401(k) retirement savings plan.

Conclusion

THE Obstacle Course is meant to be a repeatable process for candidate observation. THE Obstacle Course you design each time you initiate a hiring campaign will look very similar to the last, but will have to be tailored each time to meet the needs of your company based on the skills and traits that are part of THE Right Fit.

Remember, THE Obstacle Course is about making the best use of you and your hiring team's time by:

- getting those that definitely don't fit out of the process as soon as possible in the low-touch steps and
- deeply examining the behavior in the high-touch steps to ensure the best choice.

A well-oiled hiring machine (practice, practice, and practice THE System) will benefit you by:

- snatching up talent when it's scarce because you can act quickly and effectively for yourself,
- reinforcing your culture among your current team and molding candidates as you bring them on board, and
- producing coordination in your hiring team that will work its way into other systems of your company.

Observing behavior closely as you encounter candidates will provide the data you need to make a good choice about your next team member. The next step, though, will give you THE Proof you need to really determine if they are THE Right Fit.

Initial Actions
Begin your design of THE Obstacle Course by being clear on how *assignments* can be used to reveal the skills and behaviors you need.

If you currently have an opening you are working on filling, think about that role. If you do not currently have an opening, think about the role you most often will fill. For instance, a growing SaaS-model business will have developer roles and customer service roles needing to be filled and, alternately, a retail business will need more sales representatives.

With the full hiring team in attendance, brainstorm on a number of assignments that could be used in the process. You'll find that the team will gravitate to certain assignments. The more time-intense assignments will be associated with high-touch steps and vice versa.

Also, the number of assignments in the process will generally tie in tightly with how difficult/easy it is to assess the skills and personality traits in THE Right Fit.

THE Proof

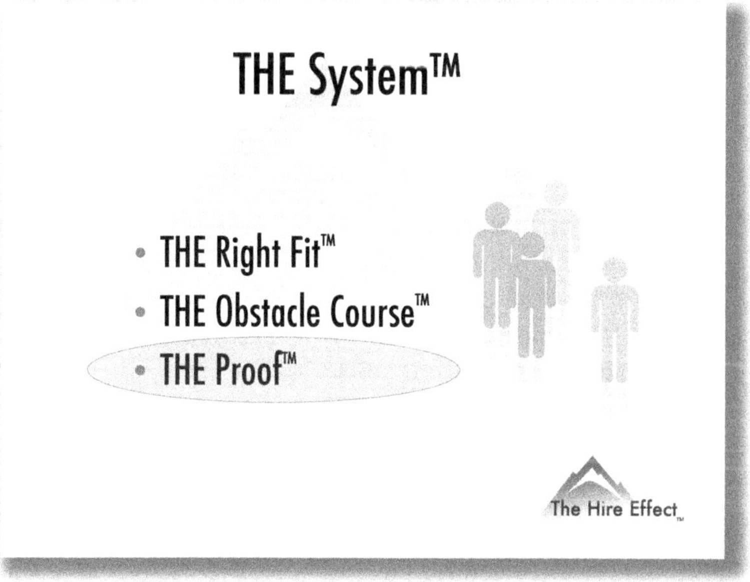
THE System™
THE Right Fit™
THE Obstacle Course™
THE Proof™
The Hire Effect™

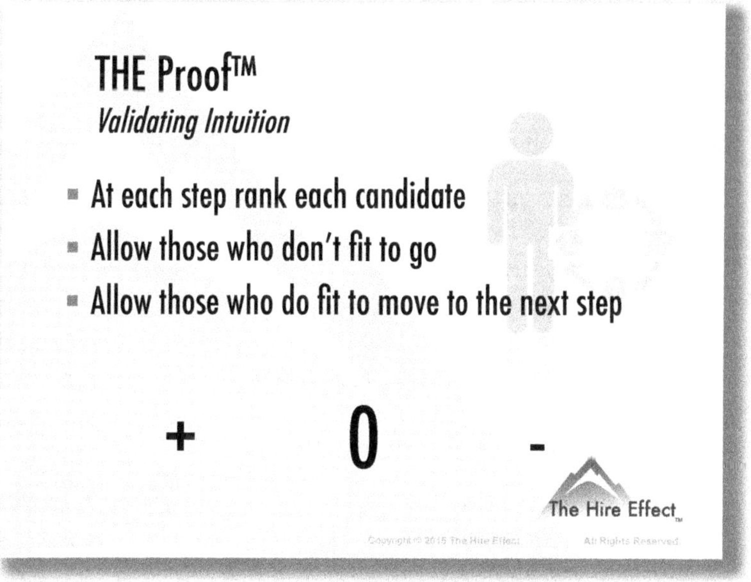
THE Proof™
Validating Intuition
At each step rank each candidate
Allow those who don't fit to go
Allow those who do fit to move to the next step
+
0
-
The Hire Effect™
Copyright © 2015 The Hire Effect
All Rights Reserved

Figure 7. THE Proof.

You know what THE Right Fit looks like, sounds like, and acts like. You've designed THE Obstacle Course to get candidates to act authentically over time, through at least three steps. Now you need a way to keep track of how each candidate matches up against each the context points in THE Right Fit and coordinate your hiring team so you can all share your thoughts. Then you need to make a good choice in the end.

The most powerful thing about THE Proof is the ability it gives you to do something called *Bless and Release*. It provides you a structure and evidence that allows you to let people go that you really like but that you've proven don't fit. It's no longer you making the choice but the evidence of an ill fit for both you and the candidate. Honestly, how many times have you encountered a candidate, liked them so much and known with a just a little niggling doubt that there was something that didn't quite fit, and then you hired them anyway?

Additionally, just because a candidate doesn't fit doesn't make them bad. They were either not experienced enough, had too small of a network to effect what you needed done or some other thing you could explain away. But you still really like them.

The thoughts along this line go something like this:

> *It doesn't matter that Matt doesn't get some of the acronyms he needs to know and he's just a little short on patience with the staff. Wow! He could charm the socks off my customers. They'd love him! So those things don't matter so much, do they? No, I'm sure they don't. He'll catch up fast enough. He'll gain the patience once he sees how it will be the best way to help our customers.*

> *Oh, I know that every other field engineer I've had that does the job well has at least five years' experience, knows all the government agencies, and has the patience of a saint working with the customers.*

I just really need this position filled now, and he's so charming. I know we can make it work!

This is the sound of you trying to convince yourself that Matt is the one for the job. Let's be honest, this is the sound of you making a bad hire.

How do you give yourself permission to NOT hire someone you really, really, really like? First, you hold them up against THE Right Fit, observe their behavior closely, and make assessments based on your observations (and those of the others on your team—let's not forget them), then you Bless and Release the people who don't fit, knowing you've made a good choice for you AND the candidate.

Assertions and Assessments
In the fall of 2004 Peter Denning released a paper called *Assertions and Assessments*. Reading and incorporating the thinking included in the paper has been instrumental in helping people to make better choices when they hire. I'm a firm believer in getting on the same page with what words mean to us as coordinating individuals. This applies to any kind of relationship and in business we are talking about your one-on-one relationships with your employees, your hiring team's relationship with one another, your sales person's with the customer, your office manager's with a vendor . . . the list goes on.

> An *assertion* is a claim about what is observable in the world.

> *Assessments* are evaluations, judgments, or opinions about the world.

It's lazy to assume both parties are on the same page about language. You know what I mean when I say "ambition", right? A slightly different interpretation can have us making very different choices without a clear understanding of why.

You and your hiring team need to share some language around this concept of *assertion* and *assessment* in order to be effective with THE Proof. Some teams decide to use "fact" and "opinion." The point is, choose words here and agree to use them consistently. You'll see in a moment how this plays into THE Proof and choosing the best candidate consistently and effectively. I'll be going with the Denning classic of assertion and assessment so we can stay on the same page.

Assessments | Plus, Zero, Minus
Remember THE Right Fit? All those context points will come in very handy here as you make assertions and assessments about each candidate. Take a look at figure . This is a tool we use for each interaction with a candidate to track each of the hiring team member's assertions and assessments.

Just to be clear, each time any one of the hiring team engages with a candidate they will use this tool. To the left are the context point reminders—in this case there are fourteen. It's important to review THE Right Fit distinctions before you start to make sure you are on the same page as the others. It is so easy to declare that you "know" them and not review them. You can start to lose sight of the shared meaning if you let go of this practice.

Your project lead team member should collect and have available at any given moment each of the Individual Candidate Tracking & Proof tools as it relates to a specific candidate. You'll get a snapshot of candidates by leafing through them.

Individual Candidate Tracking & Proof

Unique Flow Step: ______________

Hiring Team Member: ______________________________

Position: ______________________________

Candidate: ______________________________

Company Components - Culture (Values - Manners)

Populated by THE Right Fit

	+ 0 -	Assertions
Integrity		
Forthrightness		
Excellence		
Oppenness		
Casual		
Collaborative		
Peaceful		
Geeky		

Candidate Components

Populated by THE Right Fit

	+ 0 -	Assertions
Facilitation		
Industry Knowledge		
Written/Verbal Communication		
Patience		
Compassion		
Optimistic		

The Hire Effect

Rev - 111616

Figure 8. Example of Individual Candidate Tracking & Proof.

The assessments include:

- **Plus:** use this assessment when the candidate's responses and behaviors exhibit a correlation with a context point. (i.e., you see behavior and answers that show this context point is in keeping with the way they really are).

- **Zero:** use this assessment when the candidate's responses and behaviors do not give you any indication of a correlation with a context point. (What do you do if you get a zero? We'll catch up on that a bit later.)

- **Minus:** use this assessment when the candidate's responses and behaviors exhibit an indication that they are working against a context point (i.e. you see that their behavior is inconsistent with what you want in a particular context point).

Each one of the context points will receive an assessment as the candidate engages with a team member.

A brief aside is appropriate here, as I use this structure for the stages of knowing often: *familiarity, understanding* and *knowing.*[1] You will immediately be able to locate yourself in one of these **stages of knowing** as you think about different areas of your business.

You may be *familiar* with the concept of being an entrepreneur. You can pronounce it, even spell it, and describe what it is, but there's so much more depth to the topic.

You can also *understand* entrepreneurship. There are so many universities that have introduced degree programs around

---

[1] *I first encountered this model while participating in a leadership program back in the '90s. Although I cannot find reference to it anywhere now, I believe it was developed when Fernando Flores and Werner Erhard were together as students studying ontology.*

entrepreneurship in the last 5 years. After a two-year program you can wrap your head around understanding it. You get that being an entrepreneur is about innovation, commercialization, and sustainability. You can name the many components of a sustainable business.

But you don't *know* entrepreneurship until you've sweated payroll, had sleepless nights over a bad hire, or experienced the joy of winning a big contract.

When you think you know something and you are actually only *familiar* with it or only *understand* it academically, you can be very dangerous to yourself and others impacted by your choices. You are making decisions or choices based on a loose structure. You are making decisions based on something that isn't "true" for you. This is a great way to get what you don't want! Know THE Right Fit for you—everyone on your team should know it too.

Stages of Knowing

- Familiarity
- Understanding
- Knowing

The more you and your team practice, read and do things around THE Right Fit, the more you will *know* it and be able to make good decisions, support your culture, and meet needs you have by making a good hire.

Once you *know* THE Right Fit you can begin to look for assertions during the interviews. Many of your assertions will be born from watching carefully as your candidates experience assignments. Some of your assertions will come from the verbal responses they give others or whether their words match their actions.

You'll be recording those assertions on the right hand side as a reminder regarding your assessments. This practice will help you to keep the different candidates straight.

Making Core Values Assessments

Remember, core values are principles or deeply held beliefs. Simply asking, "What are your core values?" doesn't cut it, does it? Also, listing your core values and asking candidates how they feel about them is equally ineffective. (Stuff I'm sure you wouldn't do anyway.) You want to be watching for behavior that would indicate this candidate acts and holds these principles in their everyday life.

Looking back at figure 7 as an example set of core values, you would be looking for behavior that is consistent with integrity, forthrightness, excellence and openness. The candidate can clearly act in a way that is consistent with these core values AND additional core values like kindness and truthfulness. Although kindness and forthrightness can coexist sometimes, sometimes they cannot. You and your team's job is to figure out if the candidate will be kind at all costs or if he can still hold forthrightness. Can the candidate be dedicated to being truthful and still be open?

You'll be gathering assertions mainly by watching candidates' behavior as well as fully examining the language they use and then interpreting where those behaviors/language fit. The more you work on observing, writing down assertions, and making assessments as a result, the better you will get at it.

Making Manner Assessments

The majority of the way you'll gather assertions about manner compatibility is through assignments that deeply immerse the candidate in how work is done in your company. Recall that the manner descriptors you ultimately use are declaring how work is done in your company.

Your assignments in the high-touch steps will be most effective in making these assessments. Watch the behavior of candidates as they produce a blog post or write a sample customer response letter in the bullpen. Ask the candidate how completing the assignment was. Dive in and ask them how it could have been better or what they didn't like about the environment. Listen carefully for discomfort and even follow up with a dreaming question like, "If you could have the absolute perfect office to work in, what would it look like, feel like, sound like?"

You can also introduce a number of questions into the interviewing process that will get the candidate to tip her hand at her ideal work environment or environments she finds difficult to work in.

Client Experience

> *Steve, owner and CEO of a product design firm in mid-Michigan, has identified the Mood of his company with the following manner descriptors: quiet, geeky and intense. The customers they support range from a tier one advanced manufacturing company to a high end, custom bicycle maker with a small shop.*
>
> *The team was looking to add a social media guru that would be delivering both for Steve's company and also (as a value-add) for clients, providing a new line of revenue.*
>
> *Steve, rightfully so, was concerned that what he needed in a social media guru in terms of mood, skill, and personality would likely not mix well with the rest of the team. He knew that the person who could handle the day-to-day work in this environment existed, but had to suss them out prior to hiring them. Truthfully, he was afraid he'd find the person with the right skills and traits and they'd soon get bored by the culture.*
>
> *The team started with a well-written job posting calling for candidates who love a crowd of colleagues, who prefer a quiet space with an undercurrent of strong opinions that bubbles up regularly into a geek fest.*

As a result, the hiring team designed the second to last step of THE Obstacle Course so that it included a quick tour of the office and then deposited the candidate in the cubicle in which they'd be working 40 hours of the week.

They asked the candidate to construct a social media deck for the coming month using a Word doc. One of the important parts of delivering the assignment to the candidate was to not really provide much in the way of content. This forced the candidate to ask for help (more information) either from the hiring team or from those around them.

After the candidate gave the slide deck to the hiring team, they were subject to a series of questions about the experience. This assignment gave the team some great data about the candidate's skills in producing relevant content, some sense of their comfort with the environment, and how they'd react when given little to nothing to work with.

Making Skill Assessments

This is where most small businesses do a fair job in gathering assertions and making assessments. Tools you can use to gather assertions about skill often are simple exercises like the one presented in figure 8. This is an example from a SaaS company looking to find out in a low-touch step if the applicant has a basic grasp on programming principles. By including the skills testing throughout THE Obstacle Course, you'll gather plenty of assertions for your assessments of plus, zero, or minus.

Part of the beauty of a team making these assessments is that we all see different things; we all have different interpretations of what an *assertion* is. What you'll need to remember here is this is not science and doesn't need to be. The simple act of looking for assertions and then making an assessment based on something you care about will get you so much closer to THE Right Fit than if you didn't.

From: Larry No-Name Larry@NoSpam.com
Date: Tue, Apr 26, 2016 at 1:26 PM
Subject: Next Steps
To: Mia Mia@FunSpam.com
Cc: Darrell Darrell@NoSpam.com, Darrell2 Darrell2@NoSpam.com

Hi Mia,

I'm looking forward to meeting with you on Wednesday at 3:00 in our office. The interview will include members of our Development team (Darrell and Darrell) and myself. In preparation, I have an assignment for you to complete.

Please complete the following "pseudo-code" exercise.

This code is intended to handle a phone number that comes from user input. We are looking specifically at the output of localNumber. The output we want will be in the form 'xxx-xxxx' (e.g., '555-0100'). This code is a very naive implementation. Provide several examples of user input for which it will fail, and show what its output will be. Then draft an improved version, in pseudocode ('incorrect' syntax will not be penalized). We only care about the output from localNumber, but areaCode and asDigits are there to help you and you can include new implementations for them, too.

```
Phone>>areaCode
  if (self number == '') {
    return ''
  } else {
    return self number first: 3
  }

Phone>>asDigits
  if (self number == '') {
    return ''
  } else {
    return self number select: #isDigit
  }

Phone>>localNumber
  if (self number == '') {
    return ''
  } else {
    return self number allButFirst: 3
  }
```

I look forward to your timely reply.

--
Larry No-Name
President
No Spam Incorporated

517-555-3939

Figure 9. Example of a skill assignment.

Making Trait Assessments

There are many, many tools on the market to use to assess personality traits. The trouble with some is that they are expensive or require a degree in psychology to use them. Choose wisely for yourself.

If you don't have a degree in psychology, here is a bit about how THE clients usually work through this part. Hiring teams first look at THE Right Fit trait context points they are looking to assess. Hiring teams will then design interview questions and assignments that help to reveal the behavior they want to observe.

If you use no formal assessment tool and simply stay clear on the distinctions (all staying on the same page for what you mean when you say "patience," for example) and watch for assertions, you'll be much farther ahead than the average bear.

As an example go back to figure 7, where the traits are patience, compassion, and optimistic. What does patience look like? Staying in the conversation regardless of frustration with the other. Waiting through delays without getting upset. You and your team will spot the behaviors associated with patience if you are looking for them.

THE clients are all over the map with the tools they do use to assess traits. Start with what you are used to using and work with that. Each time you design a new obstacle course, someone on the team can start looking for other tools that might make sense to take on. The most commonly used tools in this area include:

- **AcuMax Index®**, which measures and reports on human wiring

    AcuMax Index® is interesting in that an expert in AcuMax will assist you in producing a profile of the individual you are looking to hire based on a consultative process. In my opinion, this process works well when you already have a group of people who are excellent in this role that you can build a profile from. Keep in mind that this doesn't have to come from within your company but can come from industry standards and reporting as well.

- **Kolbe A™ Index**, which measures the instinctive way people do things and has four components:
    - Fact Finder – gathers and shares information
    - Follow Thru – arranges and designs
    - Quick Start – deals with risk and uncertainty
    - Implementor – handles space and tangibles
- **StrengthsFinder**, which produces a profile of top strengths and how they work together

    StrengthsFinder can be highly effective in maximizing each person on your team and how they interact with one another. According to experts, this is not a selection tool. Having said that, I've seen some use it that way.

- **DiSC®**, which measures work styles:
    - **Dominance**
        - Direct
        - Results-oriented
        - Firm
        - Strong-willed
        - Forceful
    - **Influence**
        - Outgoing
        - Enthusiastic
        - Optimistic
        - High-spirited
        - Lively
    - **Steadiness**
        - Even-tempered
        - Accommodating
        - Patient
        - Humble
        - Tactful
    - **Conscientiousness**
        - Analytical
        - Reserved
        - Precise
        - Private
        - Systematic

- **Myers–Briggs Type Indicator**, which classifies tested individuals into one of 16 particular personality types produced through an assessment of these four areas:
  - Are you outwardly or inwardly focused
    - Extraversion
    - Introversion
  - How do you prefer to take in information?
    - Sensing
    - Intuition
  - How do you prefer to make decisions?
    - Thinking
    - Feeling
  - How do you prefer to live your outer life?
    - Judging
    - Perceiving

  Making assessments using this tool likely will require an expert. Just as in using AcuMax, you can build a profile and test to that. You can also find experts that will help you to implement the tool. This can get expensive, but depending upon your use and adoption of the tool company wide, it may be something you want to invest in.

An important factor in choosing what model you use is taking a look at your current team and finding out what is missing (that's part of constructing THE Right Fit). It isn't unusual for a company to choose a selection tool like the Kolbe Index, get everyone on their team to take the questionnaire, and then use that as a way of getting to know the tool.

There is copious evidence that a diverse team has significant advantages over one that is not diverse. Keep in mind, diversity as it relates to the many studies you'll find has to do with multiple factors, not just personality, including ethnicity, gender, age, and so on.

Here's another route you could take. If THE Right Fit includes a trait based on communication style like "intuitive", you could work with Leadership IQ tools to test the whole team and prospective candidates to find out which group they fall into: analytical, intuitive, functional, or personal.

You and your team can be as scientific or not with this process as your time and budget will allow. Again, the important thing here is to choose something and learn how to gather the assertions to make effective assessments.

I strongly encourage you to only make these tests and assessments one piece of the puzzle. These are not all or nothing *assessments*.

Considerations

Consideration | What to Do About A Zero

A zero assessment on occasion is fine. Too many zeros can indicate a poor obstacle course design, but introducing additional assignments can produce the plus and minus assessments you need.

For example, if Mel's team assessed a zero for both final candidates as it related to their leadership skills, introducing an additional request of the candidates to produce a leadership mission statement and pragmatic plan of implementation with a new team may get her hiring team what they need to make a plus or minus assessment.

As you and your team start to know THE System, swapping one assignment for another or inserting an in a key spot could provide critical assertions at key times.

Consideration | Building an Onboarding Plan

What is an onboarding plan? Well, it's a plan to get your new hire set up and productive. This plan can include logistical items like the following:

- Schedule
- Orientation to environment
- Personal introductions
- Team/company announcements
- Productivity setup
    - Space
    - Technology
- Role description agreement
- Expectations and goals (both sides)
- Training
- Time with knowledge holders

The first six are something you'll need to do with everyone. What we want to get at in the onboarding plan, and what you can start to build in during the last stage of THE Obstacle Course, are the resources and time you (or someone on your leadership team where time is terribly scarce) need to expend to get a particular candidate productive. How much time of your key personnel are you going to have to expend to get an employee productive? This could be incredibly valuable information to make the most advantageous choice for the company financially and for the team.

Client Experience

Remember Melissa, a business owner of a marketing image consulting company? She was able to make a key decision regarding one of the top three candidates—he wasn't taking the assignment request seriously (a good indication he wouldn't take other requests seriously).

The other two candidates produced slide decks that were both pretty compelling cases to choose them. As the final interview progressed, each of the hiring team members was completing an Individual Candidate Tracking and Proof Tool.

When the candidates were excused, the hiring team project manager, Bev, set herself up to take notes regarding the conversation and resultant decisions about how to make each candidate as successful as possible.

THE Right Fit for Melissa's company had 15 context points. Starting with the first, Bev polled each one of the hiring team for assessments. It wasn't until we got to a skill context point, Industry Knowledge, that a few of the panel had a minus assessment. With a minus assessment and a discussion around what the hiring team members' assertions were, we identified a place Melissa and her team would have to invest time and possibly training to get the candidate up to speed.

We discussed and tracked whom on the current team he'd have to spend time with and also identified training needs he would have. Melissa's time was extremely limited in the next month.

After each candidate's onboarding plan was constructed, Melissa's time turned out to be the tipping point. One of the candidates had a slightly better grasp on industry knowledge than the other. Less of an investment—and ultimately less time with Melissa—was needed by the second candidate.

Again, you'll have noticed that the effectiveness of the onboarding planning is directly related to your team's ability to stay in conversation with one another and stay focused on assertions and assessments, not on intuition.

Conclusion

THE Proof puts checks and balances in place to ensure that you and your hiring team will:

- Bless and Release when it is appropriate,
- gather assertions and document them,
- make effective assessments,
- consider onboarding costs in a final choice,
- build a stronger and more intentional culture, and
- present an effective structure for quarterly or annual performance.

Initial Actions

Looking back at the assertions and assessments section of this chapter, it may be highly beneficial for you and your team to get clear on the distinctions you need to truly share:

- The context points of THE Right Fit
- Distinctions in your industry
- Distinctions within your business's history
- Assertions and assessments
- Others?

Make a list of the words you are using, discuss and document a shared definition of what those words mean, and make sure that you publish the list for the hiring team, leadership team, and others in the business who would benefit from it.

THE Higher Effect

Well, now that you know what THE System looks and feels like and can tailor it to your company, we should talk about The Hire Effect™ higher effect.

Business is all in language, whether it's texted, emailed, written in a letter, spoken over the phone, or discussed in the break-room in person. It's all in language: the words, the tone, and the body language. What you and your employees say and talk about shapes the culture. You are co-creating the culture every day in tiny increments of time. Once you bring to life a crisp story of who you are and what you want, you are better able to look for it and choose it.

David Cooperrider, best known as the co-creator and creative thought leader of Appreciative Inquiry (AI), said something in a 2003 AI workshop that has always stuck with me. He and Frank Barrett were leading the class and the discussion topic that day was "intentional affect of doing an AI project". He said that if you get people in conversation about a positive question, and you engage the whole community, the culture shifts toward the positive.

THE System gives you a structure for bringing into language what your culture is, basing it on your core values and the mood in which the work is done. Once it's brought into existence, into language by the hiring team, discussion on your culture will expand to other people in your company—whether you introduce it intentionally or not.

Your hiring team will engage in deep discussion and agree on what your culture looks like in a person and in a group. The more each of you see it and talk about it, the more it is strengthened and the more the topic comes up in discussion organically—around the water cooler as they say.

You could be intentional about introducing the articulation of culture your hiring team produces. The context points for culture could be worked into the following:

- Weekly status meetings
- Quarterly report meetings
- Annual goal setting sessions
- Performance reviews (see below)
- Marketing messages
- Communications

Take a look at THE Performance Check-in form (see figure 9) and get a basic idea of how these conversations are guided around the context points. With each meeting (quarterly, semiannual, or annual), the employee will self-evaluate and make some *assessment* of their performance using plus, zero, or minus. In the far right column the employee will work to document assertions that will be good discussion points. This reinforces the idea that you as a community care about these context points and it provides a structure for conversation.

These discussions do not necessarily need to be formal or take significant amounts of time. They could be incorporated into a lunch discussion, during a walk around the building, after a team meeting, or as an impromptu check-in. With a normal structure of no more than 10 people reporting to any given person, these could be completed relatively easily. Also, the structure is in place should you wish to shift the culture in a given way as we will talk about on page 108 from "willing" to "proactive".

Consideration | A Compatible Leadership System
Very much in alignment with THE is a leadership system called the ***Entrepreneurial Operating System*®** (EOS). EOS is the most effective and scalable model for visioning and implementation through focused collaboration I've seen. There

are others, but this one includes something inventor and founder of EOS Worldwide Gino Wickman calls The People Analyzer.

Self Evaluate Prior to Performance Discussion or Leadership Team Checkin

Performance Checkin

Role : ____________________

Superver: ____________________

Name: ____________________

Date: ____________________

Company Components - Culture (Viaues + Manners)

THE Right Fit

	+ 0 -	Goals/Supporting Behavior
Caring		
Community		
Beyond		
Willing		
Flexible		
Supportive		

Candidate Components

THE Right Fit

	+ 0 -	Goals/Supporting Behavior
Strong Relationship Building		
Clear Communication		
CRM capable		
Self Starter		
Inclusive		
Friendly		

The Hire Effect™

Rev - 110216

Figure 10. THE Performance Check-in form.

The People Analyzer works the Jim Collins bus analogy of assessing right people, right seats. Gino sets a baseline for the core values for each position using a scale of +, +/− and −. THE works similarly but with all the context points of THE Right Fit and the discussion tool around the assessments that is THE Proof.

In figure 10 you'll see an example of the People Analyzer. This tool can be used in a number of valuable ways and focuses specifically on the importance of the core values.

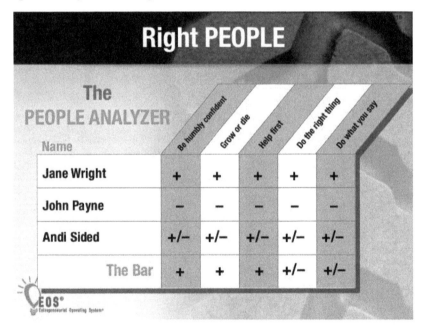

Figure 11. Example of the EOS People Analyzer.

For comparison's sake, the same core values were used in the example of THE Right Fit for Sales Lead (figure 11). You can see that the rest of the context points also are assessed in the interview conducted by Andi. There's also a slight variation in how the assessments are "scored." THE plus, zero, and minus allow for discussions on the leadership team.

Individual Candidate Tracking & Proof

Obstacle Course Step: Panel Interview

Hiring Team Member: _____ Janet Fuller _____

Position: _____ Sales Lead _____

Candidate: _____ Andi Sided _____

Company Components - Culture (Values + Manners)

Populated by THE Right Fit

	+ 0 -	Assertions
Be humbly confident	+	When she answered "My teams are dedicated and excited about our projects. Leading them is an honor. They are great people."
Grow or die	+	"I don't give up easily - there's just too much at stake. We can do way more than we think we can."
Help first	0	
Do the right thing	+	"There's no doubt, when we didn't deliver in a fashion they expected, we had to approach them and talk to them about reducing the project cost."
Do what you Say	-	Twice late for interviews and showed up unprepared for this one.
Swift and Sure	-	Felt like she was dragging her feet on the last assignment we gave her.
Forthright	+	She faced the elephant in the room earlier when she asked about the other candidates in the process. Loved that!
Open	+	When Jeff told her she need to work on her delivery, you didn't blink and said, "Thank you for that feedback and I'll work on that."

Candidate Components

Populated by THE Right Fit

	+ 0 -	Assertions
Team building	-	She flubbed around trying to come up with how she would get at what each of her team members cared about.
Visioning/Strategic	+	She brought in with her a pretty well developed vision but her implementation thoughts were sketchy
Pipeline management	+	Like I said, her implementation thoughts were sketchy. She didn't know any CRMs
Relateable	+	She told a couple stories that make her approachable. The one about bumping her head getting into her car this morning, for instance
Creative	+	Who would have thought to contact the local SCORE chapter to see if there was a research analyst on staff?! Great free resource.
Abundant thinker	-	She wasn't at all interested in a discussion about collaboration with the other divisions. It was as if we were in competition.

The Hire Effect

Rev - 111616   Copyright©TheHireEffect 2015

Figure 12. Example of Individual Candidate Tracking & Proof.

There's a strong correspondence between EOS and THE. Many of the distinctions used are based on the psychology, biology, anthropology, and ontology of business.

Gino has written and coauthored a number of books that are very easy reads and give you the feel and flavor you need to figure out if you want more information:

- *Traction*, the model

- *Get a Grip*, the story of implementation

- *Rocket Fuel*, on the relationship and importance of the visionary and integrator pairing

All of the EOS books provide an excellent view into how communications and a system in a leadership team look under their model, along with the tools invented for coordination. Additionally, you can find facilitators to help your team implement the tools, which I highly suggest.

Consideration | THE Team Assessment
Remember this?

If you aren't sure what skills and traits you actually need on the team, you'll want to take stock of what you already have. With **THE Team Assessment** comes a two-phase project that could seriously increase your team's efficiency in working with one another AND reveal the skills you need to go out looking for.

> A *role* is a high level view of or agreement on the areas of responsibility a person holds or will hold as your new employee.

Phase one of THE Team Assessment is an interview that will help to identify and make clear the roles each of your current team members play and are accountable for. You'll want to first get clear on what you mean by role—everyone has to be talking about the same thing. Remember role?

Then a series of questions will help you to shape THE Role Agreement, which will look like the example in figures 12 and 13.

Once all the role documents have been constructed and those agreements between the person holding the role and their supervisor/manager have been reviewed, signed, and are in place, each person has a clear understanding of what their role is held in common with those they are accountable to.

These role documents, along with THE Performance Check-in, can provide a structure for the kind of meaningful discussion you and your leadership team need to have with one another and others on your team.

If once phase one of this process is complete it is not evident what is missing, the completion of phase two will push the holes in your team out into the open and increase efficiency.

> **Role – *Office Operations & General Operations Support***
>
> **Phoenix Personnel Currently in this Role** – *Jaqui Allmalah*
> **This position reports to** – *Franklin Jacobs*
> *Sally O'Leary*
> **Individuals reporting to this role include** – *None*
>
> ---
>
> **Role Responsibilities**
> This role is responsible for infrastructure, logistics and visitor/caller experience in the main office. Additionally, this role provides clerical support for all services provided by the company.
>
> **Sample of tasks and duties**
> **OFFICE OPERATIONS ROLE**
> - Process incoming mail and packages
> - Greet and assist office visitors
> - Infrastructure issue support and handling
>   - Office maintenance issues
>   - Break-room maintenance
>   - Office supply ordering and inventory
>
> **OPERATIONS SUPPORT ROLE**
> - Clerical assistance for Client Fulfillment
>   - Statement of Work iteration and filing
>   - Compilation of deliver docs
>   - Monthly status report creation
> - Clerical assistance for Internal Operations (Accounting & COO)
>   - Reconcile vendor statements with Accounting
>   - Package and main payables each week
>   - Receive American Express receipts and enter into Accounting
>
> **Requirements for Qualification to hold Role**
> - High school Diploma
> - Three Years related work experience
> - Quickbooks Proficient
> - Microsoft Proficient
>
> **Metrics for Success – for goal setting**
> - % Task completion
> - Timeliness of task completion
> - Office coverage
>
> THE Team Assessment™   Copyright © 2016 The Hire Effect. All Rights Reserved.   Page 1 of 2

Figure 13. Example of THE Role Agreement, page 1.

Skills and Trait Profile
  Skills
  - Knowledge of Microsoft suite
  - Quickbooks Proficient
  - Organized
  - Good Communication (written and verbal)

  Personality traits
  - Self motivated
  - Patience
  - Diplomatic
  - Optimistic/Positive
  - Flexible in personal communications

Accountability Agreement

Reviewed and accepted role description:

_____   _____
Employee Sign   Date

_____   _____
Manager Sign   Date

Figure 14. Example of THE Role Agreement, page 2.

Phase two of THE Team Assessment involves nailing down process flows for each individual. This phase will require the following:

- A shared set of distinctions regarding process (see figure 14)
    - Situation
    - Process
    - Predefined process
    - Data (in and out)
    - Decision
    - Document
- Creation of process flows for each person, generally no more than 6 processes per person
- Review and discussion among the team to insert feedback and update loops
- Periodic updates so process flows remain efficient

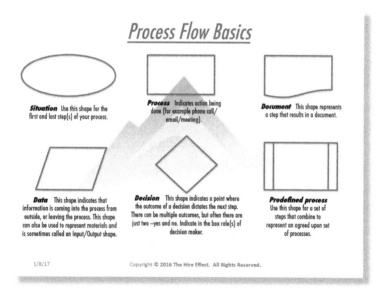

Figure 15. Process Flow Basics.

Figure 15 will make this a bit more understandable. The example is a process flow for process flow creation and updates.

Your company's process flows connected together, especially where they are each owned by different people, represent a significant opportunity to "see" and discuss how coordination can happen more fully and how you can deliver results within the business more effectively. Where two process flows come together, there is an opportunity for one or the other person to request a feedback loop or a notification loop that includes an email, memo, text, or call notifying them that the process they own will soon need to be ramped up.

If there are processes with no role owning them, there's a gap in the team.

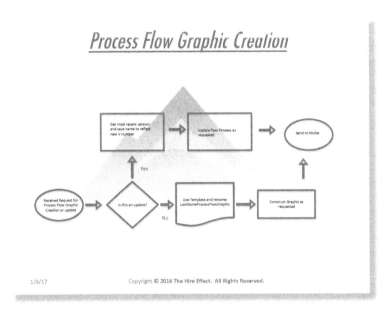

Figure 16. Example of a process flow for the creation of a process flow.

Consideration | Organizational Change

An organizational change initiative (shifting the culture of your company) can be implemented if the culture you find through these exercises isn't desirable. The more you bring your culture into clear, common language with all your employees, the easier a change initiative will be. With or without intentional conversation on culture change, it will take more time than you'd likely imagine effecting a change. You can begin a shifting of your culture in the hiring process with key hires and intentional communication throughout the process. What better place to start to change the stories than as the new team members begin employment?

> "If you want to learn about culture, listen to the stories. If you want to change the culture, change the stories."
> *Unknown*

The hiring process, in particular when a key hire is being made, is a perfect opening for the initiation of a change in the culture. Many change initiatives include tactics like monthly stand up meetings, one-on-one meetings between a member of the leadership team and individual employees, internal marketing campaigns, weekly internal announcements, and/or review and redesign of processes both external and internal. With intention and focus, everyone begins to take on new language and new behaviors and with that, the culture shifts.

First, you have to have a clear picture of what your culture is now—core values and descriptors of the way work is done, with clear distinctions for both and an idea of what each "looks" like in behavior.

Second, invent a clear picture of how that culture should change. Let's go back to figure 3 on page 33. Pretend this was a description of your culture and "willing" didn't quite represent what you were after in the identity of your company (after all, whether you want to or not you will be known and described by how people think of you). You want to shift the culture from a responding nature (action happens to us and we are eager to help) to an active nature, so you'll use the manner descriptor "proactive."

Third, discuss with your team what being proactive means—creating a situation by making something happen. Then examine and get on the same page about what behaviors exhibit proactive qualities—taking charge, recognizing potential problems, identifying solutions and acting *before* a problem arises; or, alternately, getting organized so things don't get out of hand.

Fourth, when you recognize "proactive" in a candidate that you'd like to hire, make a point of having a discussion about what you see in them that your team aspires to. That might look something like, "Jeffery, our hiring team truly appreciated how you brought solutions to make sure problems didn't arise in the assignments we gave you during recruiting. We want you to know that we aspire to that here. We are working on shifting our team behavior from one of just being willing to get something done to making sure it happens in the first place. Would you be willing to help us do that as a team by being a good example?"

Lastly, be sure to acknowledge Jeffery's behavior during onboarding to reinforce it in him and the team members he works with.

This focused and intentional set of actions will help to shift everyone's behavior over time.

Client Experience

> *Remember Mike the "messy" publisher? He, like many Enlightened Leaders, saw a change he wanted to make and set out to turn it into reality. With a change initiative in front of him aiming at confidently being able to say that the team was quick paced, humble, and organized, Mike and his leadership team found and employed a few*

strategies to reach their goal within the year: storytelling, EOS (Entrepreneurial Operating System), and THE Performance Check-in tool.

EOS got the team on the same page and out of the gate within the first few weeks by making it a quarterly rock to declutter the office and set into place a few processes making it natural for the whole team (now 101 of them) to talk about what it meant to be organized.

There were an additional three hires in that time: an office manager, a warehouse manager, and an editor. THE hiring team made sure there were questions and assignments that helped to identify the issue of messy vs. organized, looking for strong leaders in office and warehouse managers to hold the change initiative.

Consideration | Seating Your Culture
Your Unconventional Hiring Team will have a leg up on the rest of your company once a few hires have been completed. They'll have coordinated with one another, discussed with candidates and the leadership team, and put into action the culture context points over and over again. It will have become more of a way of doing their work and thinking about things than for those in your company who are not on your hiring team.

The context points, both values and manners, can be applied to every process in your business, whether high-level (sales, innovation, production and delivery processes) or micro-level (how a meeting is run, how a performance review is conducted, how a choice is made about who attends what conference, how you choose a vendor, and more).

The more cohesive your business is around the things you care about, the more you are all marching to the same drum and the more effectively you can act together. Remember, core values are your deeply held beliefs and ethics and the manner is the way in which you do the work. The beauty of this is it doesn't matter how big you get; you can still point to these context points and say, "Is what we're doing consistent with our culture?" and make course corrections if you need to. It's all about execution.

Conclusion

As an Enlightened Leader you are thoughtful and intentional about the initiatives you invest company time and resources in. With the invention of a clear story of what your culture is you can begin to shape the future. Intentional moves toward a more powerful structure to succeed use leadership systems like EOS, company wide conversations such as THE Team Assessment, seating your culture in daily conversations and the use of highly effective models like Appreciative Inquiry.

The question is, what are you doing to shape your culture into a more powerful environment to grow or consistently sustain advantage over your competitors?

Initial Actions

During your annual or quarterly team meetings, carve out some time to envision what the ideal culture for your company is and how it is consistent with what you would like your company to be and do in the next three to five years.

Start by reading through the Five Principles of Appreciative Inquiry as a group. One by one, go through the Principles constructing different ways to support the change initiative and choose some achievable number of tactics to employ throughout the year.

Below are the Five AI Principles (first developed by David Cooperrider and Suresh Srivastva):

> ***Constructionist principle*** – This principle suggests that people's actions are based on their beliefs and beliefs come from relationships. Everyday interactions construct

the organizations people work and socialize in. Inquiry is to initiate new possibilities for inventing and acting.

Principle of simultaneity – This principle suggests that when we inquire about a particular human system this begins change, it encourages people to think and talk about the question and in the process they learn and find out new things. This principle also suggests that the questions that are most emotionally charged are the questions that have the biggest change effect.

Poetic principle – This principle suggests that the everyday stories told in an organization or community are it's life's blood and those stories are repeatedly and consistently being coauthored. The topics chosen in inquiry invoke meaning and understanding. Throughout the inquiry, effort is put into using words that energize and encourage the best in people to be revealed.

Anticipatory principle - This principle suggests that our vision of the future shapes what we do in the now. Humans within a community are constantly looking to the future, projecting expectations and those are the mobilizing forces behind making a powerful and positive present.

Positive principle – This principle suggests that positive affect and social bonding are necessary for sustainable positive change to happen. Positive moods and emotions increase innovation, flexibility, and openness . They also foster stronger relationships among those participating in the inquiry.

Remember, business is in language and organizational change takes time and intention. Just talking about a more ideal culture for your company begins the transformation. Those ideas that are compelling to the group will live; those that are not, won't.

Wrap Up and Concluding Thoughts

Big companies form HR divisions that are all about hiring and compliance. You don't have the resources or personnel to do that.

Big companies have the budget to deal with hiring that isn't particularly dead on. Underperformers can shift to new positions that better fit their skills and personality traits. You don't have that budget.

Big companies also have the luxury of providing bells and whistles in their benefits packages that lure in and keep the best talent. You don't have that luxury.

Big companies employ organization change consultants that cost them hundreds of thousands of dollars to initiate and implement cultural change initiatives. You don't have the money to do that.

For far too long, small business owners have lived trying to implement the traditional big company hiring practices with what budget and personnel they do have.

Getting clear on what you need, using the resources you have to their fullest potential, and making dead-on choices every time will serve you well no matter what size your company becomes.

Hiring should always remain a leadership function. The leadership team should be significantly involved with your Unconventional Hiring Team:

- Ensuring a coherent story for new employees about the vision
- Helping to support a great culture by hiring for it in the first place
- Holding the hiring team accountable for getting the best talent possible for your company

- Taking the opportunity to shift the culture when necessary

Know what you want and need from a new team member. If you don't use The Hire Effect to construct THE Right Fit, use something else. Making a choice without knowing what you want, significantly increases the chances of a poor hire.

Take your time looking at the prospective candidates. Hire slow and fire fast. Taking the time to observe, assess, and choose the right candidate pays off so much more in the long run.

Bless and Release those that you know aren't a right fit but you so, so feel compelled to hire either because you like them or because you really want to do a friend or family member a favor. Make sure the fit is right for you and it will be right for them too.

Appendix A

Example of a Campaign Status Document

THE Proof™ - Campaign Status Document

Considering
Not considering

Responsible party		Sienna (Indeed, Monster)	Sienna			Bonnie			Michele		Michele			Michele Josh Stan
Candidate Name	Application Submission Date	Michele (Employee outreach)	Response 1A or 1B Sent	Assignments complete	Step 2 Date/Time Arranged	Assignment Complete	Response 2A or 2B Sent	Step 3 Date Arranged	Assignment Complete	Response 3A or 3B Sent	Step 4 Date Arranged	Assignment Complete		Response 4A or 4B Complete
Vickie P.	1/20/17		1/21/17	y	1/21/17									
Meredith F.	1/20/17		1B											
Tammy R.														
Donna U.	1/23/17		1B											
Venita D.	1/25/17		1B											
Neakia P.	1/30/17		1B											
Kenta R.	1/30/17		1B											
Stacy Lynne G.	1/30/17		1B	y	1/30/17	Y	2A							
Katie W.	1/30/17		1B	y	1/31/17 - 10 a.m.	y	2B	2/9/17 - 10:30 a.m.	y	Sent 3B	2:13.17 - 10:30 a.m.	Y		Made offer
Kathleen K.	1/30/17		1B											
Joseph S.	1/30/17		1B	Y	1/31/17 - 10:30 a.m.	y	2B	2/3/17 - 3:30 p.m.		Sent 3A				
Khadijah A.	1/30/17		1B	Y	1/31/17 - noon	N	2A							
Lori B.	1/30/17		1B											
Kristie S.	1/30/17		1B	y	2/2/17 - 1:30 p.m.									
Deborah B.	1/31/17		1B											
Deborah K.	1/31/17		1B											
Darlene R.	2.6.17		1B	y	2.7.17 - 9 a.m.	y	2A							
Heather G.	2.6.17		1B	y	2.7.17 - 9:30 a.m.	y	2A							
Audrey B.	2.6.17		1B	y	2.7.17 - 10 a.m.	y	2A							
Julie B.	2.6.17		1B	y	2.7.17 - 10:30 a.m.	y	2B	9.17 - 11:45 a.m	No	Sent 3A				
Candice H.	2.6.17		1B	y	2.7.17 - 11 a.m	y	2A							
Michelle W.	2.6.17		1B	y	2.8.17 - 8:45 a.m.									

Copyright(C)The Hire Effect Feb 2016   2/19/17

Appendix B
Example of a Hiring Timeline

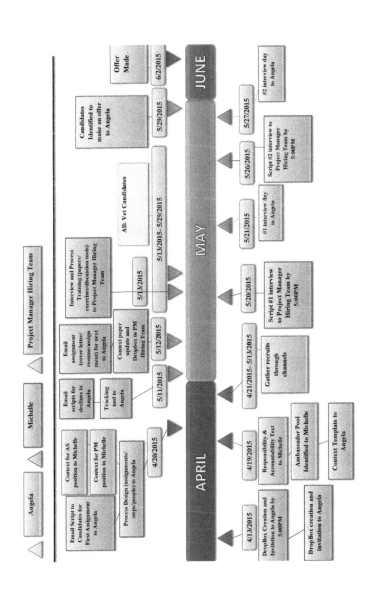

Appendix C

THE Certification is an education and mentoring process for small businesses to make full use of THE principles. An assessment is performed to determine the roles and responsibilities of your current team, an Unconventional Hiring Team is identified, and they are trained, mentored, and ultimately connected with other THE Certified teams.

THE Certification includes the following:

A two-day training and tailoring of THE Tools:

- Day 1 Training
    - Conversation for Action review and practice
    - Hiring team role identification
    - Development of the hiring timeline for the current open position and training on how to develop future timelines
    - THE Right Fit tailoring
- Day 2 Training
    - THE Obstacle Course tailoring
    - Opinions and THE Proof
    - Design for communications (scripts)
    - Tracking and Performance Tools
    - Interview Training and Practice

Ongoing Mentoring and Training through:

- Huddle calls
- One-on-one Coaching with Team Members
- Final interview participation

Appendix D

An Observation in Listening

Choose one day-long, non-working period (from rise in the morning to sleep at night) in which you observe these basic rules:
- You may not speak unless:
    o you are observing basic niceties such as thank you, please, you are welcome, hello and goodbye, etc.
    o you are making basic listening noises or words such as "I see", "okay...", "hmm", etc.
    o you have been asked a question - in which case you may only simply answer the question but no more
    o you are asking questions. Likely the conversation will be very awkward unless those questions are **open ended**
- You must arrange before your day of observation to meet a friend for coffee, lunch, dinner on the day of observation
- You must run at least 1 errand that day (grocery shopping, pick up a book from the store, etc.)
- You may answer the phone if you'd like on that day, but you must observe the above rules

I anticipate:
- you will want to lead with your questions. Be careful to not ask questions that reveal your judgment or opinions. So a question like, "Did you explain what a total idiot she was being?" would be leading. More appropriate would be, "What did you think of her actions?"
- that some of you with spouses or house mates will have someone ask you, "What's up?". You may tell them, because it's a question! But only if they ask. Your answer should be brief and to the point, "I'm working on listening better." (So if they say, "You're acting weird." That's not a question. You can though, ask them a question such as, "Can you tell me a little bit more about what you mean by

weird?")
- that you may have something happen in the day that seriously makes you want to stop the Observation. If you do, ask one question, either of yourself or of the person you are interacting with at the moment. You may find that you can ask another, and yet another, and work through the want to stop.
- you may fall off the wagon. That's okay. As soon as you notice you have, jump back on.

At the end of the day or the next morning reflect on these few questions:
- What was surprising about the Observation?
- What did you find out about your conversation mate you likely wouldn't have if you hadn't been following the rules?
- What kind of meetings at work would you choose to follow these rules?
- What would it be like to engage in this conversation when both people are following the rules?
- Would it be helpful to do this again? Or periodically?

Distinctions

assertion. A claim about what is observable in the world.

assessment. An evaluation, judgment, or opinion about the world.

assignment. Anything you ask the candidate to do for you in the interview process.

Bless and Release. The conscious choice to not hire someone you really like because of the evidence showing they are not THE Right Fit for you.

choose. To consider the whole picture, and, in any given moment, select a different end goal or different tactic to reach the goal you have.

Conversations for Action. A trust building and coordination model invented by Winograd and Flores.

context point. Each one of the components of THE Right Fit is a context point.

core values. Principles, ethics, and/or deeply held beliefs.

culture. A combination of core values and the mood within which work is done.

decide. To kill off or not consider other possibilities as you move toward an end goal.

Enlightened Leader. Someone who seeks help, empowers his team, is a lifelong learner, commits to professional growth for himself and his employees, commits to process, and holds himself and his team accountable to reach goals.

Entrepreneurial Operating System (EOS). a leadership system invented by Gino Wickman.

high-touch step. a type of step in THE Obstacle Course that will take more of you and your team's time and, with that investment of time, will build the proof you need for the best match possible.

knowing, three stages of. The three stages of knowing are familiarity, understanding, and knowing.

low-touch step. A type of step in THE Obstacle Course that will be low impact on your hiring team's time and quickly identify those candidates that clearly are not a match for THE Right Fit.

manner descriptor. A word that describes how the work is done in any given company. A number of manner descriptors make up the mood of the company.

mood. The portion of the culture that is the combination of all the manner descriptors used to describe how the work is done.

power. Your ability to achieve the things you care about, like taking care of your family, reaching professional goals, and helping people and organizations in your community. Often power has a negative connotation in today's language. Wherever the word "power" is used in this book, it is a factual assessment.

role. a high-level view, or agreement, of the areas of responsibility a person holds or will hold as your new employee.

THE Certification. an education and mentoring process for a hiring team, that when complete, has fully incorporated The Hire Effect principles.

THE Proof. a set of tools wherein, after comparing a candidate to THE Right Fit, the hiring team members make assessments of a plus, zero, or minus against each context point.

THE Obstacle Course. a step-by-step process all candidates will encounter fully that includes low- and high-touch steps and assignments.

THE Right Fit. a clear point by point description of the perfect candidate for a particular role.

THE Team Assessment. a review by The Hire Effect personnel of your current team to determine if people are in the most effective role for the company and if there are any gaps in the team.

THE System. THE Right Fit, THE Obstacle Course, and THE Proof, as well as THE Tools used for implementation of The Hire Effect.

Bibliography

@harvardbiz. "Diverse Teams Feel Less Comfortable - and That's Why They Perform Better." *Harvard Business Review*. N.p., 2016. Web. 11 Dec. 2016.

@RecruitLoop. "75 Behavioural Interview Questions To Select The Best Candidate." *Do Better Hiring – The RecruitLoop Blog*. N.p., n.d. Web. 12 Dec. 2016.

"Appreciative inquiry." *Wikipedia*. Wikimedia Foundation, 06 Feb. 2017. Web. 14 Mar. 2017.

"Kolbe Corp." *Kolbecom Event*. N.p., n.d. Web. 31 Dec. 2016.

"The Myers & Briggs Foundation - MBTI® Basics." *The Myers & Briggs Foundation - MBTI® Basics*. N.p., n.d. Web. 31 Dec. 2016.

"Top Employee Assessment Program - Tools, Services for Employers." *AcuMax Index -*. N.p., n.d. Web. 10 July 2016.

"What is Appreciative Inquiry?" *David Cooperrider*. N.p., n.d. Web. 02 Jan. 2016.

"Your Life's Path." *DiSC | DiSC Personality Test | DiSC Profile | DiSC Assessment | DiSC Test*. N.p., n.d. Web. 31 Dec. 2016.

Denning, Peter. "Assertions and Assessments." *Denning Institute*. N.p., Sept. & oct. 2004. Web. 10 Dec. 2016. <http://denninginstitute.com/pjd/TT/AssertAssess.pdf>.

Murphy, Mark. "Which Of These 4 Communication Styles Are You?" *Forbes*. Forbes Magazine, 2015. Web. 31 Dec. 2016.

Rath, Tom, and Barry Conchie. *Strengths-based leadership: great leaders, teams, and why people follow*. New York: Gallup Press, 2008. Print.

Winograd, Terry, and Fernando Flores. *Understanding Computers and Cognition: A New Foundation for Design*. Norwood, NJ: Ablex Corporation, 1986. Print.

Worldwide, EOS. "EOS - Entrepreneurial Operating System for Small Businesses." *EOS - Entrepreneurial Operating System for Small Businesses*. N.p., n.d. Web. 03 Mar. 2016.

THE Author and Founder

Miche Rayment has been designing human systems for change since the late 80s at Chevrolet's Customer Assistance Center. Change initiatives since then have included Regional Entrepreneurial Collaboration for the State of Michigan, Great Lakes Entrepreneurs' Quest, and her most recent initiative The Hire Effect™ (THE). Through THE System, Miche's work to effect change is focused on building high performing teams laser focused on culture and skill.

Working with startup and growth-focused businesses and using THE System, Miche is working to change how small businesses think and do hiring, in part by giving business leadership an actionable way to talk about and choose the right people for their teams.

For years—over 20, but don't tell anyone—Miche has been designing programs and events that allow business owners to meet one another, incorporating change oriented forms such as Appreciative Inquiry, World Café, and Open Systems through artful facilitation where everyone is heard, everyone engages, and the collective knowledge is used to design change for the betterment of everyone.

www.TheHireEffect.com

What are our Core Values?

What is the Mood of our company? What manner descriptors clearly identify that mood?

What process do you currently have that allows you to match for your culture?

What would be a more powerful Mood for our company?

How do your current employees use your core values to shape their work?

What will you do differently to find a match for your culture now?

What initiatives would help you to shift the mood of your company over time?

What process do you currently have that allows you to match for the skills and personality traits you want in a new employee?

What will you do differently to test candidates for skills and personality traits now?

Who should be on my hiring team and what role would they play?

How will you organize your hiring team so you work well together?

How will you incorporate experiential interviewing into your hiring process?

How vulnerable are we to making a bad hire? What are the costs of a bad hire for us?

How will you train your hiring team so that they are watching candidates' behavior and making effective assessments?

Do we really need to hire someone now? What can we do to increase our efficiency? Make the most of our current capacity?

Are there roles no one on the team is accountable for?

How can we get better at Blessing and Releasing?

What assignments will you be using to "test" your candidate pool now?

What are you doing to keep your hiring team on task to hire in a timely manner?

Where are you deciding when you should be choosing? Where are you choosing when you should be deciding?

How many steps do you generally use to assess a candidate? Is that enough? If not, what will you do differently now?

How well do you and your hiring team listen to your candidates?

What will you do to build the listening muscle in you and your hiring team?

What are you doing now to prepare for an interview? Are you treating it like an interruption to your day or an important initiative you need to take time with?

What do you need to do to hire slowly enough but not too slowly?

What do you need to do to take swift action when you know you need to fire someone?

What are you doing in your job postings that will be appealing to the right people culture wise?

What are you and your hiring team doing to check your gut?

What are you doing to free up your time but staying involved enough in the hiring process?

What kind of personality trait assessment models make the most sense for your company to use?

What are you doing in your hiring process to reveal a personality that is a good fit for your team?

What are you doing in the hiring process that could be used in the on-boarding process?

What are you doing in your hiring process that gets the candidate thinking about getting productive quickly?

Do you have a sense for how your culture needs to change to meet your vision for the future?

What will you do to begin that shifting in the culture now?

Do you have a leadership system that helps you hold your employees responsible for their roles and hold them accountable for goals?

Does each of your employees know exactly what their role is? Have they committed clearly to holding that role?

How efficient is your team? Do you have excess capacity?

Are you ignoring your culture?

Do you have clear practices in all your core processes like sales, marketing, delivery that orient around your core values?

What are you doing to explore new markets? How does that translate into your team evolving? What new hires do you need to make this year?

Just how many questions is this woman going to ask?